God Bless

AUTHOR
* * of * *
LIBERTY

AUTHOR
✦ of ✦
LIBERTY

My Story of America

Dr. Michael T. George

A POST HILL PRESS BOOK

AUTHOR OF LIBERTY
My Story of America
© 2016 by Michael T. George
All Rights Reserved

ISBN: 978-1-68261-145-6
ISBN (eBook): 978-1-68261-146-3

Cover Design by Quincy Alivio
Interior Design and Composition by Greg Johnson, Textbook Perfect

PRESS
Post Hill Press
275 Madison Avenue, 14th Floor
New York, NY 10016
posthillpress.com

Printed in the United States of America
1 2 3 4 5 6 7 8 9 10

The young Sergeant led his troops through the jungles of Vietnam. They had walked for miles when the brave soldier began to feel somewhat uneasy. A nudging, invisible voice kept telling him to get rid of the explosive devices he was carrying in his vest pocket. At first he tried to ignore it, but a divine sensation began to overwhelm his thought process. He walked a few more steps before finally throwing the explosive items into the jungle. He felt crazy for doing it, but hopefully now he could march on with a clear mind. Minutes later a mortar landed directly in front of the young Sergeant. The explosion sent shrapnel ripping through his legs and torso. He fell to the ground severely wounded, but alive. Had he not thrown away the explosives he was carrying a few minutes earlier, that would not have been the case. Had he ignored the Providential warning he would not be here and neither would I. Thanks Dad for listening to that still, small voice, may you always remember His grace upon your life.

Acknowledgements

My deep appreciation goes out to those brave men and women who were willing to risk everything to travel to a world they never knew. Their voyage aboard the Mayflower set forth a series of events that would change the world. It would do us well to remember their purpose for establishing a colony in the new world.

In the name of God, Amen. We whose names are under-written, the loyal subjects of our dread sovereign Lord, King James, by the grace of God, of Great Britain, France, and Ireland King, Defender of the Faith, etc.

*Having undertaken, **for the glory of God, and advancement of the Christian faith**, and honor of our King and Country, a voyage to plant the first colony in the northern parts of Virginia, do by these presents solemnly and mutually, in the presence of God, and one of another, covenant and combine our selves together into a civil body politic, for our better ordering and preservation and furtherance of the ends aforesaid; and by virtue hereof to enact, constitute, and frame such just and equal laws, ordinances, acts, constitutions and offices, from time to time, as shall be thought most meet and convenient for the general good of the Colony, unto which we promise all due submission and obedience. In witness whereof we have hereunder subscribed our names at Cape Cod, the eleventh of November [New Style, November 21], in the year of the reign of our sovereign lord, King James, of England, France, and Ireland, the eighteenth, and of Scotland the fifty-fourth. Anno Dom. 1620.*

Foreword

*A*uthor of Liberty has taken me down a road I feel I have been before. The day my F-16 was hit with a missile over Bosnia, requiring me to eject from my plane, landing in enemy territory, my life changed forever. For the next six days I had to survive on my training, my instincts, and most importantly my faith in God. There were times I wondered if I would ever see my family again. It is during these times of adversity where your faith becomes real.

My own story is one of courage, faith, and patriotism. This is exactly what you will experience as you move through these incredible stories of eight amazing individuals. Their chronicled feats of bravery, perseverance, faith, and dependence on God are truly extraordinary.

The sixth item in my military code of conduct states, "I will never forget I am an American, fighting for freedom, responsible for my actions, and dedicated to the principles which made my country free. I will trust in my God and in the United States of America." I believe after you read through these memorable events you will see how this statement above truly sums up this book in a nutshell.

Focusing on family, faith, and freedom, Dr. George picks up right where his best-selling book, "My Story of America," leaves off. It is an adventure through the lives of the people who make America an incredible place to call home. In a day where America has strayed from her founding principles, this work will renew your spirit and give you a clear vision on how to overcome the difficulties life brings your way. Few books have the power to change a person's life, but these inspiring stories accomplish that very task.

—Captain Scott O'Grady USAF (Veteran)
Author of *Return With Honor,* New York Times Best-Seller

And the Rockets' Red Glare

As the security officer opened the laptop he began to diligently search the hard drive for any incriminating evidence of financial wrongdoing. File after file was reviewed with every document and note being heavily scrutinized. Jackpot! The picture now blazing across the screen revealed a nine-year-old secret. The issue of theft was no longer a concern. The official looked closely at the man featured in the center of the photo. He knew the face and he knew it well. There could be only one option, the man in the picture must be put to death. I am the man in the photo and this is my story.

The foul stench of war filled the air of the streets where I lived. My eyes slowly opened as I heard the noise of men killing men echo through the alleys of the town I called home. The tiny room where I slept was cluttered with bodies of others sleeping on the floor. There was no such thing as a bed in my world.

I was born in 1983 more than 7,000 miles from America in Kabul, Afghanistan. My childhood would best be described as one of survival. For me it all began in the year 1991, when civil war broke out in my homeland. The Mujahedeen, also known as the Islamic Fighters, took over the city of Kabul where a power struggle immediately ensued. Seven different groups all vying for control of the city turned my life into one of heartache and anguish.

Men mercilessly killing other men all based on their ethnicity. Communities broken, lives destroyed. Neighbors who were once friends, were now pitted against one another in a fight to the finish. It was an un-civil war of the highest degree. The media called it, "An ethnic struggle," I called it, "insanity."

We were a humble family with very little to call our own, yet we had been content with our lot in life. For years my family lived peaceably on the northeast side of Kabul in a province occupied by people of Tajik descent. We were all friends and neighbors, common people with a common goal; survival. The war changed it all.

My family was not Tajik. Before the war, this had never been an issue, but now we were viewed as the enemy. We were forced to move to the other side of the city into a different province. I wept. It had been the only home I had ever known. Unfortunately leaving my home would be something I would have to experience far too often.

Each night, terror raced through my mind. I wondered if I was going to see the morning sun. I wondered if I would live to see another day. It is not a feeling I can adequately describe, but those who have experienced it, know it well.

Precautions were always made wherever we lived to protect us from the hazards lurking in the streets of our province. In the back of our home we had an area known as a safe room in which we piled blankets and pillows. I remember a large, heavy blanket placed over the window for protection.

Looking back I think how silly it was for me to think that a simple blanket covering a window would bring me protection, but I believed it would and since I am telling you this story, maybe it did.

Every day I spent most of my time in the safe room. Every window covered, every door bolted shut. I was a young boy living in a place where I could not see the outside world. Yet I could plainly hear the sound of fighting all around. It truly was a picture of hell.

I remember specifically on one occasion, when in the middle of the night a rocket's red glare shot across the sky and exploded in the air near our home. I could hear the thunderous roar of the bombs as the warring factions engaged one another.

I was terrified. My only thought was to head to the basement for protection. Immediately, my younger brother and I raced down the steps. I just knew we would be the first to arrive. Our family dog however won the race and for all intents and purposes it looked like he had been there for quite some time. Maybe they are not such dumb animals after all.

The basement contained its own hardship. For the most part it was a safe place, but it always had a few unwanted visitors; very nasty, very large scorpions. Because of this fact, my brother always slept with his shoes on. He did not want to try to look for them in the middle of the night when the bombs were going off. Unfortunately for me, I did not always find my shoes in time. On more than one occasion I was stung by the scorpions. Truly, not a pleasant experience to say the least.

Going to school was another challenge during this time of war. It was not uncommon for us to be in school for only two weeks and then have it shut down for months because of the fighting. It was certainly not a good learning environment. It is probably the reason why many Afghan people are uneducated today.

After enduring this hardship for more than two years, my family decided to send me to live with my uncle in Islamabad, Pakistan. This was not uncommon in the region in which I resided. Families would often relocate a child to a more peaceful area so at least one heir would live in case the rest of the family was killed. Since we were living in a war torn-city with death occurring daily I totally understand why my father sent me away.

My uncle was a hardworking man. He toiled for months on end to produce the vegetables he would sell on the streets of Islamabad. I would be another mouth to feed, but also another laborer for the fields. The work was hard, but my life was peaceful. I no longer had the fear that death was just waiting outside my door.

I split my time between working and attending the school Pakistan established for refugees. I was working hard, getting educated, and sending money to my family back in Afghanistan. It was a difficult existence but I finally had a stable environment to call home.

On a few occasions I went back to Kabul to visit my family, but the danger I encountered was harrowing. The city was being destroyed little by little due to the constant fighting of the seven groups struggling for power and control.

However, in 1996 all that would change as a new group came to power bringing peace to my homeland. Well, we thought they were bringing peace, but how wrong we were. When the Taliban gained control everyone was glad because the fighting between all the ethnic factions came to an end. Folks were throwing candy in the streets to celebrate the Taliban's rise to power. With the war over it was now safe for me to come home. I went back to Afghanistan to live with my family.

This feeling of peace would not last long. We soon realized things were about to get much worse. Yes it was true the war had ended, but the Taliban's way of rule was detrimental. They brought a very strict version of Islamic law known as Sharia into our region of the country.

Imagine if you will what it is like for a young boy to walk down the road only to see the body of a dead person hanging from a pole in the middle of the street. Also, since their law required someone who stole to have their hand cut off, it was not uncommon to see human hands dangling from the wires hanging above the road. Blood would run down the severed hand where it fell into puddles on the dust covered road underneath. Packs of dogs were always roaming the city looking for a meal of rotting human flesh.

The Taliban had no compassion. They were a brutal, savage group of people who would turn on their own without conscience. In fact, one of the fighter pilots for the Afghan army had refused to bomb an innocent village, so the Taliban had him hung by the neck from a crane. They paraded his dead body through the streets of Kabul for all to see. They did this for several days. They wanted to strike fear into the Afghan people. Their rules and penchant for evil was unfathomable.

These abusive individuals took every opportunity to rule with an iron fist. I remember one sunny afternoon while returning home from buying a few vegetables at the market I was stopped by the Islamic Police. My heart thumped rapidly as they walked around me as a wild animal stalks its prey. They looked closely at my head discussing amongst themselves the issue at hand.

Before I knew it I felt a hand grab my arm, then another man from behind grabbed the other. The vegetables I had purchased fell to the ground as I struggled to free myself. A large barrel shaped figure wrapped his arms around my head putting pressure against my neck. I could feel my ability to breath was being cut off.

My eyes caught a flash of light as it reflected off of the metal cutting device the man held in his other hand. I could not make out what he had and I did not know what was in store for me. I had committed no crime yet now I was about to endure their abuse. I felt the blades as they made their way through the top of my hair. I heard the men laugh as they watched clumps of hair mixed with blood fall to the ground.

The abuse endured for what seemed like hours but in all truth was only minutes. After the Islamic Police had successfully cut a stripe down the middle of my head then another stripe across the top from ear to ear they dropped the cutting instrument to the ground. The barrel shaped man released his grip and stepped back to admire his handiwork. He laughed as he gave the word to his men to begin my beating.

After multiple blows to my body and several to the head I laid on the street broken and bruised. I soon learned I had committed a crime; my hair was too long. It was against Islamic law for a man to have long hair so they administered the required punishment.

I would like to say that events like these were rare, but they were a regular occurrence in our country. If you were not in a Mosque for prayer time they would beat you mercilessly then drag you into the Mosque for the time of prayer. I can remember being beaten one day because I was walking with my mother and sister. Under the rule of the Taliban, it was against the law for a man to be out on the street with a woman that was not his wife, sister or mother. The Islamic Police however would pounce on you first then ask who the woman was that you were with. Beat now and ask questions later was their unwritten motto.

This time in our country was very bad for the boys, but it was much worse for the girls. A woman was not allowed any longer to attend school under their regime, nor could they have a job or career. The Taliban considered them to be useless property.

The situation in the city became ruinous and poverty was rampant. There was no work and no jobs available anywhere. Even the people in the rural area of the country struggled. The only crop they were allowed to grow were poppies; hence the opium trade skyrocketed under the Taliban.

Everywhere throughout the region people struggled to have any kind of food. The normal everyday comforts which most of us take for granted such as electricity and telephone service were non-existent in the area where we lived.

To make matters even worse, many homes in our province consisted of women who had children, but whose husband had been killed in the civil war. They were in such a terrible predicament. Since the Taliban outlawed women from holding any job, the only way they could earn money for food was to turn to prostitution. Of course this was strictly prohibited. Women who were caught were often brought into the town square where they were publicly stoned until dead. For many women it did not matter the consequence, because it became the only way they were able to feed their children.

Things were so bad that prostitution was higher during the Taliban regime than it had been during any other time in our country.

I knew personally of about fifty families where a mother had children and the father had been killed in the war. Since they could not work because of the Sharia Law, they were left with nothing to do but sell their bodies. Some women even had to result to selling some of their children into slavery just to take care of the remaining babies at home. I can't even imagine the agony the mother went through when she had to choose which child was to go.

Women were also especially vulnerable to the risk of kidnapping. If the Taliban or Islamic Police saw a women they liked, they would just come and take her away. They did with the women whatever they pleased. Young girls would be raped repeatedly then often killed once they grew tired of them. Everyone during this time lived in terror of what the Taliban might do next.

Everyday life was getting heinous so my father made the decision to send all of the family to live in Pakistan with my uncle. He remained behind and worked on the streets in Afghanistan as a money exchanger. His job was not sanctioned by the government because they had their own exchanging houses that were corrupt. Because my father exchanged Afghan money for Pakistani currency at a fair rate people would do anything to locate him. Unfortunately, on more than one occasion, the Taliban also found him. The beatings they delivered were indescribable, but it did not deter my father. He took seriously his responsibility to care for his family. He was willing to endure whatever punishment they brought his way.

Before we moved to Pakistan my brother and I would help our father with the money exchange. During the winter it was very dangerous because of the subzero temperatures we had to endure. My brother would sit outside on his bicycle with the money hidden in a basket. My father would enter an establishment and seek out someone needing his services. Once a customer was found he would bring them outside to my brother where the transaction would take place. Unfortunately, my brother ended up losing many of his fingernails and a few toes due to the frigid conditions. Despite all of this, he never complained. He felt like he was doing what he needed to do to help his family survive.

The winter weather was so brutal it was not uncommon for the city or province to be shut down for a month at a time. Trying to travel was almost impossible, but we always seemed to find a way to get where we needed to go in order to buy food.

In the beginning, when we moved to Pakistan, it was a welcomed change. Even though we were refugees, we were treated with respect. We could attend school and my family could work. Unfortunately, after a while the situation began to change. The Pakistani police began to harass us. It was not uncommon for them to take our money and leave us beaten in the street. Even folks from Afghanistan who had a visa and passport soon become the targets of their unjustified brutality. We were easy prey because of our different look and language. It did not matter that we were human beings created in the image of God, to them we were just easy targets.

To be perfectly honest with you, I did not feel like I was human. I felt like I was just an object meant to be beaten, harassed, and victimized. Life seemed to have no purpose until hope appeared on the horizon in the year 2002.

★ ★ ★

Hope appeared in camouflage, wrapped in body armor, with a big beautiful patch of stars and stripes. The United States military came to Afghanistan and everyone knew the Taliban's rule of terror would soon be over. These brave patriots delivered to us a freedom few would have ever expected could exist in our lifetime.

I am sure there are some people who did not like the aspect of this foreign invader coming into our homeland, but for most of us they were welcomed with open arms. It would be a chance for us to live in peace, without fear.

Not only did they bring the anticipation of freedom, they also brought the conveniences of life most Americans take for granted. In Afghanistan I had never lived in a home with electricity, in fact, most people in my village did not have electric. We also never had a phone. We always had to go to our neighboring country of Pakistan if we wanted to make a phone call. Clean water, good roads, and television were next to arrive. I, as well as most people in the community, were overwhelmed.

The United States military had brought hope to us. In my country there were no female doctors. In fact, girls were not even allowed to attend school. Now, because of the influence of the United States, you could go throughout the country and find schools available for girls. It was just such an amazing transformation. When I look back, I get so disgusted at all the unjust media coverage that painted the American soldier as a ruthless warmonger. The hope which came with those men in fatigues is something which cannot be talked about enough. My life was changed because they came.

With the overthrow of the Taliban at hand, my family immediately moved back to Afghanistan where we were re-united with my father. By this time I had graduated from high school in Pakistan, so I enrolled into Kabul University to continue my education.

My father felt that it would be good for me to study English since we were seeing a large influx of English speaking people coming into our country. He knew they would need translators and the opportunities would be endless.

He was so right, within no time I was working part time doing translation services for foreigners. My English was not great, but I knew enough by this time to be able to help people go into a shop and purchase items or food.

My time at the university was so valuable, each day I became more equipped to be an experienced translator. Before long I could speak and read English proficiently. With this ability I was able to land a job with a local tourist organization offering translation services to visiting foreigners. Afghanistan has a five thousand year old history and people from all over the world came to see the treasures of antiquity. Before long, American-based companies began working in the country and I was offered a position to provide English speaking tours of my homeland.

I enjoyed taking visitors around the area. Whether it was the northeast, the northwest or the city center, I knew the places the folks would want to see. The security of the region had improved drastically, so traveling was no longer the danger it had been. The United States military had brought stability to our region and most of us were very grateful.

My life would take another new twist when in 2003 I met a couple from the United States who were teaching in my country as volunteers. This would turn out to be a very dynamic relationship. Since I had grown up during the war there were two things I understood; survival and revenge. Forgiveness was not a trait I practiced nor had ever experienced. Yet this couple interacted with me in a way which was truly foreign. They loved me like I was their own son. How could strangers from a foreign land behave in such a manner? The question was one for which I had no answer.

Not only did I become their tour guide, they also hired me to be their personal driver. I escorted them around the countryside pointing out the historical sites of Afghanistan and would translate any interaction which occurred with the locals. One of the main areas needed for translation would be when we stopped for food.

There are two kinds of restaurants in Afghanistan; one for the locals and one for the foreigners. The price difference is astronomical. For example, a dinner for two in a local restaurant would cost about two dollars, however in the restaurant for foreigners it would cost one hundred dollars. A lot of it has to do with the requirements for food handling to foreigners, but some of it was just price gouging.

Normally, as a tour guide, I would always wait outside while my customer went in to eat. Once they were finished they would come back to the car. Then we would continue the tour. However, this couple from the United States was quite different in their approach. They insisted I go into the restaurant with them. Then to my stunned surprise they paid for my entire meal. This was totally out of my realm of experience. Never had I ever had people treat me with such respect and kindness.

I did not understand what was happening. This couple was different from anyone I had ever met in my entire life. They were not only kind, but they showed me forgiveness when I would make mistakes. I would say to them, "I am sorry." They in return would say, "There is no reason to be sorry, it was a simple mistake. Now let us teach you the right way." I was blown away by their love to me. No one in my family ever forgave me for my mistakes. That was not the culture in which I was raised.

All of their love, kindness, and forgiveness reached a boiling point in my life. Why were complete strangers being so kind? I knew I had to find out the answer. One day I turned to them and asked, "Who are you people? I mean, what do you believe?" In a moment of hesitation they looked at each other, unsure as what to say. Then with a boldness few could understand they reached toward me and placed in my hands a Bible.

This was such a risky move on their part because I was Muslim. Fortunately for them, the Bible they gave me was in the English language. Had they given me a Bible in my native language I could have had them arrested. It is against the law in Afghanistan to give a citizen a copy of the Bible in their native language. Foreigners can have a Bible in their own language but even just having a Bible in the Afghan language is strictly prohibited with punishment by death.

Regardless, I was intrigued with the gift. Certainly something in this book had the answers to my questions about this couple. If they knew the secret to love and forgiveness then I wanted to know it as well. With smiles on their faces they stated, "You will find the answers to life in this book."

Since I had been studying English I could read it quite well and could not wait to delve into this book of mystery. When I arrived back home to my family I decided it would be best if I kept this gift hidden from the others.

I did not have a room of my own. There were several of us who all slept in one room. We had no bed so we just laid on the floor. I had one of those lights you could strap to your head which was used for reading so when nightfall came I laid down on the floor and covered my head with the blanket. With the light strapped to my head I opened my new book. Since I had no clue where to go or what to read I just flipped to a page somewhere past the middle of the book. Laying on my back with the book held above my face, the light was able to shine effectively on the words.

Now as I began to read in the eighth chapter of a book called John my mind transported me back to a time when I was a child sitting at a soccer game inside Kabul stadium. Everyone in the stadium was so excited and cheering on the home team. The contest was very competitive. It had reached a fevered pitch when the game was abruptly stopped.

The entire stadium went from intense excitement to a moment of panic as the Taliban leaders came onto the field. An announcement was made over the public address system indicating that every door had been locked and no one was to attempt to leave.

Fear gripped my heart as a man, bound and gagged, was brought forth into the stadium. The Islamic Police forced the man down onto his knees. I could not believe the words I heard blaring across the loud speaker. "This man has been accused of murder and according to the law he must be executed."

Without any warning two members of the Islamic Police held the man in place as the Taliban took a large knife and severed the man's head from his body with forty thousand people looking on. It was a hideous and gruesome sight; one which is implanted in my mind to this day. A living breathing human had just been brutally killed in my presence and it was all I could do not to vomit.

Next, a woman was brought forth into the stadium. It was announced to the crowd that she was caught in adultery and according to the law she must be put to death. The Taliban had stones brought to them. Within minutes they began hurling these agents of death at the helpless woman. As each stone made contact with her frail young body you could hear her cries of anguish. Within moments, her bleeding, lifeless body dropped to the ground. Another dead person now laid in the middle of the grass field where only a short time earlier a game of recreation had been played.

The lifeless bloody bodies of those who were just executed were then dragged across the grass field. The announcement was then made that play would now resume. The image of men kicking around a soccer ball while running through the blood stained field was sickening. Did these people not understand the great atrocity which had happened right before their eyes? Was there no love for their fellow man to be found anywhere in my homeland?

As I remembered this instance from my childhood, I turned back to the book I had been given only to read a story that seemed all too eerily similar. In this book of John a group of religious leaders brought a woman to Jesus who was caught in adultery. Their intent was to have her stoned because according to the Law of Moses she had committed a crime punishable by death. At this very moment I stopped reading and thought to myself, "Well, if they stone this woman then there is no difference between me and them. If this is what the American's believe, they have nothing different so I will just give them back their book."

As I focused my eyes back onto the story I noticed a very different ending from what I was accustomed to. Jesus basically told them, "Whoever here that is without sin, they can cast the first stone." This giant nugget of truth hit me like a ton of bricks. There would be no one who could cast a stone at the woman because all of us are guilty of sin. We are all guilty of doing wrong. It did not matter if I was Muslim, Hindu, Buddhist or Christian, I realized we are all sinful. We are all in need of someone to rescue us.

Reading that story from the book of John began a journey for me which would last for three years. Then finally in 2006 I turned my life over to the Son of God. My life was changed forever. I remember the day when in a private home in Afghanistan I publicly declared my faith in Jesus the Christ.

It was a very warm day as several of us gathered for Bible study and prayer. Sitting around the room in this small home were folks from the United States, the Philippines, Argentina, and Afghanistan. It would be in this same house where I would be baptized with several other Christians in attendance.

The air in the room seemed fresh with a newness I cannot describe. As my body disappeared under the water it was as if I reappeared a new person; the old me had passed away, replaced with someone brand new. In the jubilation of the moment, one of the men took my picture to commemorate the occasion. It would later be that image that would almost destroy my life forever.

Becoming a Christian may have changed who I was on the inside, but my circumstances remained very much the same. I could not publicly declare my faith in Afghanistan. In fact, it was against the law for me to have converted from the Muslim faith. So every time it was required I still had to go to the Mosque for prayer and attend every Muslim ceremony.

I am sure you can only imagine what it was like to sit listening to someone expound one falsehood after another and not be able to say anything. I was certainly in a quandary. However, I found myself having a greater love for my fellow man than I ever had before. In fact, I was thinking constantly on how I could show the love of Christ to my friends, neighbors, and even the person sitting next to me at the Mosque. I began to earnestly put forth the principle taught by Jesus, "To love your neighbor as you love yourself."

I also began to ask questions in a challenging way to those around me in order to get them to consider what they were so blindly following. For example, I had a neighbor who was a Mullah, which is like a preacher in the Christian faith. He was sixty-four years old and had four wives, the youngest one being eighteen. One day I asked, "If I should grow old and marry several women with the last one being very young, what is going to happen to them when I die? They are not allowed to have a job so who is going to take care of them?" He could provide me no answer. I was so desperately trying to show how we were living in a culture of persecution against our women and the Muslim religion was propagating it.

Every day was like a new beginning for me. I had been rescued, set free; yet my fellow countrymen were still enslaved in a religious system which brought them no hope. They blindly followed, never questioning the dangerous principles which lead to the poverty and persecution of our people. I could plainly see how God placed a value on women and yet I was living in a culture which viewed them as nothing more than objects to be used and abused.

The hardest part of my new found faith was that I could not openly share it with my family. I knew I wanted them to have the same peace as I, but to openly come forward would mean instant rejection and banishment from their presence. Each day I determined to figure out a way to show God's love to them.

In a large family it is not uncommon for family arguments or bickering to reach a boiling point. Our family was no exception. In the past I would join in the argument, now I found myself becoming the mediator. I would provide a solution to the heated confrontation which they never would have thought of before. Since I had a totally new mindset, I would come up with the solution God wanted instead of relying on my false beliefs from the past. The wisdom was not coming from me, it was coming from the Bible. The insights were astounding and to me, they made perfect practical sense.

What you have to understand about the Afghan culture is that we are an un-educated people. We would blindly follow whoever was in charge. So when a person in authority tells us what to do we do it. We do not ask questions? Since accepting Christ, I had a new perspective and looked to God for direction, rejecting the foolishness of what evil men were telling me to do.

During elections people voted for a candidate even though they knew he was a murderous thief just because he was a member of their tribe or lived in their community. Nobody would take into consideration what is right versus what is wrong. This is the reason we are always in trouble. I imagine there are parts of America where people blindly follow one political party or another because their family or area does. They don't ask the question what is right or wrong, they just blindly follow. This is much like what takes place in Afghanistan but on a larger scale.

Now that I was a follower of Christ my mindset changed. I was able to look at a situation with totally different eyes than I had in the past. To illustrate this point I will share with you an episode of heated argument which occurred in my family.

My younger brother had gotten into a physical fight with my cousin. Before long my uncle and his entire family showed up at our home. Sides were being drawn. On one side you have my entire family and on the other side you have my cousin's entire family. Things were getting very heated.

At this point I stepped forward and asked, "Who is the elder in the room." My uncle stepped out and said, "I am." I took my cousin, brother, and uncle and made everyone else leave the room. I looked at my uncle and said, "Don't ask them who is at fault; they both are. Tell them they are not allowed to fight with each other. We are a family, we love each other."

My brother piped up, "No it is his fault." Immediately my cousin shouted, "No it is his fault!" I quickly stated, "No, you both are at fault. You both are guilty because you fight. We do not fight in this family, we love each other and stand by each other."

I now turned to my uncle and said, "Ok, you tell them what they are going to do. They are either going to be friends or they are not to speak to one another again." My uncle knew the right answer. I had just laid it out before him so he turned to me and said, "You tell them what to do."

I looked at them both and said, "You are to forgive each other for what you have done. Then go forth and be good friends from today." Almost miraculously they looked at each other and apologized. This was such a different outcome then what would have normally taken place. Before I met Christ I would have been ready to beat my cousin to a pulp because he hit my brother, but after my life change I could look at the situation clearly and see that forgiveness was the answer.

Within minutes everything was great and my uncle came away looking like a man of wisdom because he solved the problem. Deep down we both knew what took place, but I did not want the credit. I was trying to plant the seed of God's love into their hearts.

After graduating from the university it was time for me to become married. This is the basic custom in my culture. My marriage was arranged for me. I did not meet my wife until the day before I was to be married. Even though it would be a huge risk, I knew I had to be honest with her from the very beginning about my faith in Christ. I can clearly remember pulling her aside and saying, "I am not a Muslim; I am a Christian." Remarkably she said, "I do not care, I know that you are a good man and you help everyone in your family."

In September 2007 we were officially married according to the customs of the Muslim religion and my culture. In my mind this was basically done for show. I knew deep down that I wanted to have a

Christian wedding ceremony where we pledged our lives to each other in the presence of God. This was no contract, it would be a covenant.

Of course we could not just come out and do this in public, so in January of 2008 we had a secret ceremony before a preacher with several of my Christian friends in attendance.

Our marriage truly was an interesting dynamic. In Afghanistan whatever a man says a woman does. They are not viewed as equals. The man is always the head and the woman is the servant. Being a Christian I wanted to show my wife how I was different. I wanted her to see how I valued her as an equal. She was not to be my servant, but to be my partner with whom God had blessed me.

At this point I had never asked her if she was a Christian because I knew she would just go along with whatever I said. Remember, in Afghanistan the woman does or says whatever the man wants. It is totally a subservient culture where the value of women is greatly diminished.

My wife would now begin to experience a new way of life. Our house soon became an underground church. Each week several people would come to our home for prayer and Bible study. My wife would graciously serve them, never once being disrespectful or even worse turning us over to the authorities. Had she wanted she could have had us all thrown into prison for blasphemy. That would have meant certain death.

I was enjoying my work as a tour guide. I was meeting incredible people from all over the world on each journey I would take. On one occasion I took a lady from Texas to see the giant Buddhas in Bami-yan. She was so grateful for my help and knowledge of the region that soon we became friends.

She was a leadership trainer for an organization that helped the Afghan people become better leaders. She invited me to come to one of her sessions. They were conducted in the home where she was living in my country. I decided I would go to see what it was.

The session ended up being quite good. In fact it totally impacted my life, so I asked her, "Why do you want to do this for the Afghan people?" She answered, "Because it is something everyone needs." I knew then that I would love to be connected with such an organization.

There was only one problem, she did not have any money to pay me to help her. In fact, she had been doing it voluntarily. However, within about two months she contacted me and said she would love for me to help her with the leadership sessions.

I was very interested, so I met with her for a formal interview. During our time together she looked at me and said, "You make very good money at the job where you work and I cannot pay you like that, so why would you leave there to come work with me?" I looked at her honestly and said, "It is because this is what my people need." Becoming a Christian gave me an even greater love for my people. That may sound strange to some, but to those who have experienced this life renewing power, it makes perfect sense.

The next day I went to my boss at the tour company and told him of my plans. He understood, but first requested that he meet this lady from Texas. He did not want to lose me to someone who did not have my best interest at heart. My boss was from North Carolina, but lived in Afghanistan.

After he spoke with the lady, he came to me and said, "I hate to lose you but I believe this is the best place for you to go." How right he would be.

The next week I began working as the office manager for the organization. We were doing our training sessions in her living room at the time, but within five months we were in a building with fifteen rooms and twenty-five employees on staff. We were making a difference in my country. From 2008 through 2012 we trained over 4000 Afghan government employees on the topic of servant leadership.

During this time, I went through a leadership academy in order to become a trainer with the organization. From there I worked my way up to partner with the company and then shortly thereafter I became the head of security.

I was meeting so many people who were going on to be prominent leaders in the new Afghan government. My position as head of security with the leadership organization led me to interact regularly with the Afghan police force. Since I was bringing in foreigners from the United States to work in the country as leadership trainers, I had to get the security permissions from the appropriate authorities. Our organization was training many of the people who worked doing security within the Afghan government. I became very well known within the international community in Afghanistan.

Dealing with the Afghan government proved to be a challenge. No matter what you attempted to get done, someone somewhere wanted a bribe to make it happen. If I needed to get documentation for a foreign worker I was asked for a bribe. If I needed a work permit, I was asked for a bribe. This was something I would not do. The policy in my company was no bribes, so quite often I ran up against obstacles that were difficult to overcome.

I continued in this position for the next few years and every day my life was getting better. By now I had been blessed with two wonderful children, a boy and a girl. My wife and I were growing closer together as a couple and after a rough childhood my adult life was on a successful track. Nothing could go wrong now; my, how deceived I was!

★ ★ ★

Everything began to fall apart the day an engineer with a construction company from the United States was arrested for some financial problem with his company. The man was from America and any portion of impropriety was immediately questioned.

His confidential papers, items on his person and his MacBook Air laptop were gone through with a fine tooth comb. As the Afghan police began their search, the picture they found on his laptop would mean the peaceful end for my existence in Afghanistan. For you see, this was no ordinary engineer. This was a man who had also been at my baptism and had innocently snapped a photo of my conversion to Christianity. This picture would be my death sentence.

The Afghan security forces knew me and they knew me well. To them I had committed a crime punishable by death. I had betrayed Islam. I was a blasphemous traitor deserving execution.

You can imagine my surprise when the Afghan police, many of them I had trained, showed up to arrest me. When the American man's laptop was placed before me with my picture of baptism I knew there was nothing I could say. My nine-year-old secret was now out in the open. The look of hatred in their eyes was more than I could bear. I knew what would happen next and it would not be good.

Immediately, I was taken to Islamic authorities where I was locked up. Within the hour my torture began. Their plan was to have me tell them every Afghan I knew who had converted to Christianity. They also wanted to know what foreigners were secretly working in the country as missionaries.

As the officers entered my cell with AK-47s in hand I was not sure what to expect. Then, without warning, the back end of a rifle slammed into the side of my face causing two teeth to be dislodged. Another blow left my eye and the side of my head swollen and bleeding.

The verbal abuse which occurred with every strike contained words and insults I do not wish to share. However, I am sure you can easily imagine the hate which spewed from their mouths. This would be the beginning of their plans for my torment and suffering.

Next I was restrained in a chair as they brought jumper cables into the cell. They attached the cables to my fingers and moments later I felt the electrical shocks course through my body. I convulsed, sending agonizing screams through the cell. Insults and laughter filled the air as they mocked my existence and the love I had for Christ.

Without warning, I was struck in the face, spit upon, and kicked relentlessly. The question asked of me was this, "Do you plan to give us the information we want?" When I answered "no" the electrical shocks began again. With each moment of torture they promised to stop if I would only give them the information they wanted. I knew I would never give in. I knew in my heart that my God is greater and my God is stronger than anything they could do to me.

When the electrical torture did not succeed, I was placed into a locked cell with ten other prisoners. They tied my hands behind my back telling everyone I had betrayed Islam. For the next several hours those men beat me until I could hardly move. Every hit, every kick, every brutal taunt and blow somehow reminded me of what Christ must have gone through during his time of torture and eventual crucifixion.

For the next four days I would endure more beatings, electrical shock, and torture. I knew eventually the tortures would end and death would come. The physical abuse I endured could not compare to the emotional abuse I sustained when they showed me a paper declaring the marriage to my wife was null and void. The government declared our marriage over as they issued a decree of divorcement. Broken and battered, I laid in my cell wondering if I would ever see my two children again. All I had worked for was gone. As tears of extreme sorrow ran down my face I thought to myself that death would most certainly be a welcomed friend.

On the fifth day, I surmised my day to die had come. At the door of my cell appeared a man I knew quite well. However, he was not there to execute me, he was there to let me go. This man was from my village and rather than have my execution for Christianity bring reproach on our community, he would prefer to have me go free. He wanted no one to know that someone from his village was a traitor to Islam.

As he opened the cell door he vehemently breathed at me, "Don't let me ever see your face around here again or you are dead." I was stunned, yet I was not so sure I was out of the woods. As I left the prison I was waiting to feel the piercing quiver of a bullet in my back. Often a prisoner would be released only to be shot in the back as they exited. Yelling voices of, "He is trying to escape," would usually fill the air right before it happened. This way they could get away with killing you without having to explain it to the government officials or the media.

As soon as I was out of sight I immediately made arrangements to get out of the country. I knew at this point I could not return home, nor could I return to my family. They would not accept me since I was a Christian.

I headed north to Tajikstan to stay with a German doctor I knew. When I arrived he saw the results of the terrible beatings I had endured. Immediately he began doing everything he could to help me get well. As soon as I was able to travel I headed back to Afghanistan to get my children. All I could think about was them and my wife. Upon arrival I learned that my father-in-law had custody of my children and the decree of divorcement the authorities had issued was official. I had no legal standing to see those who meant the most to me.

I was now a man without a home, a family or a country. My own family who raised me had abandoned me. Deep down I knew they still loved me, but they could not accept me any longer because of the culture. If they were to invite me into their home it would mean death for them. The Islamic law states that if anyone leaves the Muslim faith their punishment is death. Everything and everyone I held dear in my life was now gone. It felt like I had nowhere I could turn.

★ ★ ★

Through events I can only describe as truly amazing I was reunited with the couple from Georgia who had given me the Bible. After sharing with them all I had gone through, they worked tirelessly on my behalf to get a Visa from the United States embassy.

In June of 2012 I left my homeland and touched down on American soil for the very first time. The state of Georgia became my new home. It was certainly a drastic change from Afghanistan. The people, the landscape, and the homes were amazing.

I wasn't sure what to expect in my new homeland, but the community in the locale where I settled rallied around me. I began attending church with the couple who helped me get to America. I soon found several folks willing to lend a hand. One gentleman helped me get a job, another assisted me with a car and a place to live. The love of these folks was overwhelming. I was humbled at their generosity.

I was determined to work hard to earn a living, but I was completely resolute to do everything I could in getting my wife and children back. If it meant giving my blood, sweat, and tears every day, then I would hold nothing back.

Living in a foreign land thousands of miles away from the ones you love proved to be a challenge. Even though I had new found friends, there were other people in the area who were not quite sure about this stranger from Afghanistan. On one occasion, my place of residence was burglarized and my laptop stolen. Oddly enough nothing else of value was taken.

Later it was discovered that a local man had stolen my laptop because he feared I was possibly a terrorist. He wanted to see if I had some secret terror plot planned for their town. It was so frustrating to me, but I tried to understand his misperception about the situation. I had seen firsthand what terrorists do to a city so I understood his fear.

There were however, very good people who also lived nearby who were willing to help me every way they could. I had found friends here in America who bent over backward to help me. I was determined to be united with my wife and children; they were willing to assist me anyway they could.

The things which occurred in that first year were incredible. It was amazing what was accomplished. I met people who had contacts with Christians all throughout the Middle East. These dedicated folks were willing to risk their lives for my sake. It was truly amazing what transpired. I would love to go into more detail but due to the security concerns of the people involved I cannot.

For more than a year I knew I had to get my family out of Afghanistan and into India. Even though I was divorced from my wife and the custody of my children had been transferred to my father-in-law, their lives were still in danger.

In fact, even to this very day I wake up with the knowledge my life is at risk because of my conversion to Christianity. According to the Islamic traditions I have betrayed Islam. Any Muslim who is to kill me will be rewarded by going to paradise, which is the Muslim equivalent of Heaven. Of course there is no truth to it, but like I stated before, they blindly follow.

During this time, money was very tight, but I knew I had to get the funds together to get my family to safety. I sold everything I owned; my car, my TV, and any possession I had accumulated which would fetch me some cash. By doing these things I accumulated part of the money needed to fly them out of the country to India. However I was still several hundred dollars short. My faith was certainly being tested, but my prayers were answered when a dear friend in Georgia gave me the rest of the money I needed to get them out of the country.

I was amazed at the love I saw in action. Every time I had a need, God brought someone along to assist me.

Having accumulated all the money I needed, I wired it to my family and before long they were on a plane to India. Their lives would no longer be in danger. Now a new problem would arise, they would need money on which to live. My work was just beginning.

Since I had sold everything I owned, I took an opportunity to travel to Virginia where I was told I could find better work near the Washington, DC area. I was willing to do anything and go anywhere to make sure my family had the money they needed to survive.

When I arrived in Virginia I met a man in a church who offered me a place in his home until I could get my own place to live. Then a nice gentleman from Lebanon gave me a car and said I could pay him in three months. Within a very short time I had not only one job but two. During the day I was working with a Catholic charity who helped persecuted refugees from other countries. Then in the evening I was working for Papa John's, the pizza company. Both companies treated me very well and I was thankful to God for the blessings in my life.

Providing for my family to live in India was okay for the moment, but my ultimate goal was to have them join me here in America. All I could think of was to be re-united with my wife and two beautiful children. It was nearing almost two years since I had last been able to hold them.

Some friends of mine began to help me go through the process of getting approval for my family to come to the states. It took some time, but after much work I managed to finally get the necessary approval. There would be one major problem preventing them from coming to America; they had to go back to Afghanistan to get the necessary Visa documentation. This would be extremely risky because going back meant they would be putting their very lives on the line.

Because of the danger involved, my family could not go back to Afghanistan in the normal route, we had to sneak them back into the country. No one was allowed to know they were coming; not their family or even mine. It was too dangerous.

Accomplishing something of this magnitude would take some planning and teamwork. Fortunately, I had some friends in Afghanistan who were able to make this happen. I cannot go into the details about how we accomplished this due to safety reasons, but many people risked their lives to get my family back into the country.

The next obstacle was a medical examination. My wife and two children were required to have this before a Visa for the United States would be issued. Each examination would cost four hundred dollars. Once again I sold everything I had in order to come up with the twelve hundred dollars needed to pay for their physicals.

Life was certainly not easy, but it was worth it. I did not care what I had to sacrifice for my family. Their safety and our re-unification was all that mattered to me. From the time I left Afghanistan until the day I finally saw my wife and two children again more than two years had passed. The day they stepped off of that plane and onto American soil I was never so thankful for the blessings of God. A new life could now begin!

When I first arrived in America I had so much hatred for those people who had tortured me. I knew I would always be in slavery to them unless I could forgive them, unless I could get them out of my mind. One morning as I looked in the mirror I prayed to God and said, "I forgive them, after all they were only doing what they knew." They had never experienced the love of Christ in their lives so how could I expect them to treat me any different. Deep down they are slaves to a system which does not understand forgiveness. They aimlessly follow leaders who take them down a path to destruction. Truly the blind leading the blind.

I now have a better understanding of what Paul the Apostle meant when he wrote these words to the church at Galatia, *"Stand fast therefore in the liberty wherewith Christ hath made us free, and be not entangled again with the yoke of bondage."* To not forgive them would mean a return to the slavery which had beset me my entire life. I was once lost, entangled in a system of hate and revenge, but due to the courage of a couple of unsung heroes of America I became free.

The Star Spangled Banner states that America is *"The Land of the Free and the Home of the Brave,"* and to me that statement is true. However in my mind it is better stated, *"The Land of the Free because of the Brave."* I would have never known life and truth without all the people who were willing to put their lives on the line for my sake. From the soldiers who fought the Taliban to the couple who shared their faith, these people changed my life forever.

I believe everything that has transpired in my life can best be summed up by John the Apostle, *"and you will know the truth, and the truth will set you free."*

The Bombs Bursting in Air

My heart thumped ever so slowly as a lump entered my throat. Cold and clammy sweat rolled down my forehead and over my brow. Every breath was a struggle as the organs in my body began the shutdown process. I wanted to live and I needed to live. Yet, there was only one option available to save my life. Any normal person would take it, but for me the choice was not one I could consider. In fact, it was something I believed would be worse than death. My name is Rickard and this is my story.

I guess from the very beginning I was meant to go to war. In fact, my whole family was bred for battle. My great grandfather came to America in 1860 from Austria. He was a short man with a very long beard who worked as a chimney sweep in his home country. He worked hard and lived a simple life. That all changed the day he found a stash of money hidden in the chimney of an old abandoned house. There was only one thing to do and that was to head for America; the land where people went to start over.

His timing was not the best because he ended up arriving at the beginning of the American Civil War. In 1865 he fought for the Union Army and his battles would take him all the way to Cumberland Tennessee. Hanging in my basement, I have a picture of him in his uniform. It is quite interesting to read the vital statistics, information about his heroism, and acts of bravery during the war.

Then there was my father, he was a tank commander under the command of General Patton during World War II. The atrocities he experienced led to a mental breakdown of sorts. The ravages of war can scar a person like none other. He was so disturbed at one point he went into the middle of the German Autobahn and brought the traffic to a standstill.

My older brother joined the service and was a member of the Strategic Air Command. He fought in both the Korean and the Vietnam War. I like to tell him he is a Koretnam vet. My younger brother went into the service in 1970. He was stationed in Thailand where he ran several bombing missions into Vietnam. He came home a different person. I guess you really can't imagine what it is like to send a B52 bomber out on a mission and having it never return. I assume he felt like he sent those men to their deaths.

Every family has a legacy and the military certainly was in my blood. I remember as a small child running through the woods throwing rocks at my brothers when we were in the midst of our neighborhood war games. On one important mission, several of us guys gathered in the woods behind an area where they were building new homes. There in our wilderness were several pieces of loose lumber we fashioned into a fort. For weaponry, we cut pieces of inner tube from old tires and attached them to the trees. We built a massive slingshot and we were prepared to battle our enemy. We took some hedge apples and placed them in the slingshot. As we pulled the weapon back and let it fly, it soon connected with our target; the men working on those new homes.

The battle was soon over when the men discovered what we were up to. We got into a lot of trouble because of what we did. My first experience of jungle warfare ended in defeat. There would be many more battles in those woods over the years. All were harmless and mostly good-natured fun. Too bad all my battles weren't that way.

★ ★ ★

I have fond memories of my childhood, however, when I became a senior in high school my carefree days as a child began to change. Due to the financial struggles my parents were facing during this time, I got a job with a local aircraft company in the town where we lived. I would go to school from eight to three each day and then would go to my job from four until midnight. It was not a difficult job, but it was one I did enjoy. I worked there my entire senior year and when I graduated, I knew it was time to take my next step in life. It was time I became a Marine.

Even though deep down I knew what the dangers of war brought both physically and mentally, I knew I was destined to be in the military. While growing up, I had a friend who went everywhere with me. So when he joined the Marine Corp I knew I would do so as well.

Before my graduation from high school in 1967 I made my way down to the local Military Entrance Processing Station or MEPS. There was a long line waiting out the door to get in. Young men from everywhere came to join the service. When I finally got inside the door I met a couple of the drill instructors who were there helping with recruitment. They were such nice guys; they told me about how we were going to be good buddies and drink beer on the weekend. Boy, that all changed once they got us to sign our names on the dotted line.

During that time period, my older sister who lived in Florida was having some health issues, so my mother went down to help her. When my mom returned, she was not at all happy to find I joined the Marine Corp. But what could she do, I was eighteen years old and no one was going to tell me what I could or could not do.

Well, that is not totally the truth, but it is something a young man likes to say. The fact was, my draft number was coming up. I was a 1A, so I knew I would be heading to Vietnam anyway. I figured if I was going to go I wanted to go with the best and in my opinion that was the Marines.

Right before classes were scheduled to end and my time as a student in high school was about to close, the teachers arranged for all of us boys who joined the service to come forward to be recognized. I thought it was a fitting and touching tribute to guys they figured they might not ever see again.

That summer of 1967 was my last summer at home. I spent those three months just trying to enjoy life. Hanging out with friends, taking those last camping trips, and just good-natured fun occupied my every waking moment. On August 27th my entire family saw me step aboard the plane that would take me to boot camp. Everyone believed I would return, but the goodbyes were still very heart-wrenching to say the least.

When the plane touched down in San Diego, we were met by the Marine Corp bus. They packed us in like a bunch of sardines. Across the back of the bus was one long seat and the guy who sat in the middle had another person sitting on his knees. Then on that guys knees was another guy and another and another until the entire aisle was filled with guys. I can only imagine how each guys legs must have hurt.

It seemed like such a long trip to the base, but as soon as we arrived, we knew our lives had drastically changed. The drill instructors were screaming for us to get off the bus. My buddy was one of the guys who had a guy sitting on his knees, so when he got off the bus his legs were shaking. The drill instructor walked over to him and with several other choice words said, "Why are your knees shaking?" My buddy replied, "Well, if you had just ridden all the way from the airport down here with someone sitting on your knees your legs would be shaking too."

Crack! The sound echoed through the air as I watched my buddy hit the ground. I guess the drill instructor didn't like his tone or his answer. Things were quite different back then. As we all stood in line with our feet on those yellow foot prints they had on the ground, I began to think to myself, "Maybe I have made a big mistake."

They quickly marched us into the barracks where they began to shave our heads. Every stitch of clothing we had went into a bag they would ship back to our homes. They issued us our uniforms and all night long we spent running. In fact everywhere we went we had to run to get there. My buddy who was flattened in the beginning, spent every day complaining. I figured since I was here I might as well make the best of it. I knew for sure I did not want those guys pounding on me. So I did my best to keep a low profile.

While we were out on a six mile run one day, my buddy suddenly fell to the ground grabbing his ankle. Well, in the Marine Corp you positively don't just stop, so we had to keep running in circles around him. Some guys were kicking him and yelling for him to get up. My buddy cried out, "I can't, my ankle is busted." Before long the drill instructor came over and yelled, "Son, your ankle better be broke." Within minutes the medics came and put him on a stretcher. The next time I saw him he was on crutches. His ankle had been broken in several places. It was so bad he had to be discharged.

Getting accustomed to this new environment was not easy, but a note from home always helped the situation. My girlfriend would often write letters to me and on one occasion she included a little piece of candy. Whenever letters arrived at the base, the drill instructor would always shake them to see if something was in there. When he discovered the piece of candy hidden in the letter, it was not good for me. The next thing I knew, everyone in my company had to do pushups while I ate this piece of hard candy. Needless to say, that did not go over well. So in my next letter home I said, "No ifs, ands, or buts! Do not ever send me anything!"

Getting fed was another remarkable adventure. I had never eaten so fast in all of my life. You had to get in there, grab your food, eat it, and get out. Somehow, they managed to make the fat guys skinny and the skinny guys bigger. It was always amazing to me because in the end we all ate the same thing.

After a while, I began to feel like a Marine. We began to march everywhere and if we made any little mistake we would immediately be sent to lay in the sand. The drill instructor would come along and make it rain sand all over us. Then they would run us back to the barracks where we had to get in our beds. The sand was everywhere. Within the next hour, a full inspection would take place. We had to make sure there was no sand to be found anywhere or we failed the inspection. Needless to say we got to the point where we could march flawlessly.

My next stop was the Camp Pendleton rifle range. They were taking a lot of snipers over to Vietnam and I was there with the rest of the guys to qualify. I had nothing against being a sniper, but I just felt like it was not for me, so every few shots I would deliberately throw a round so I did not have a perfect score. I could not handle the idea of being out there by myself. I did not want to be alone in the jungle.

At the end of boot camp it was time for us to get our Military Occupational Specialty which would tell what service we would perform for the Marine Corp. As they went through soldier by soldier, the only words I heard were 0311 which meant infantry, but when they came to me they said, "0331." I said, "What is this?" The drill instructor turned and said, "You are a machine gunner. You will be firing the M60. Your life expectancy will be six seconds in a fire-fight." All I could think was these guys did not like me very much.

After boot camp was complete, we headed to Basic Infantry Training. Over the course of several weeks I learned to shoot different types of weaponry. During this time they put me through machine gun school where I became very accustomed to my M60. In fact, I became so good I broke the Marine Corp record on pre-qualification day and I tied the record on qualification day for the M60. They told me when I came back from Vietnam I would be a machine gun instructor. I really thought how great that would be, but I could not get the thought of those six seconds of life expectancy out of my mind.

I made a lot of good friends at boot camp. Unfortunately, I know where very few of them are today. Whenever I remember a name, I first go look them up on "The Wall" to see if their name is there. I shed a tear when I see a name I recognize.

I made one really good friend during boot camp. He was from Michigan. We always talked about going back to where his family was from and building some cabins where people could come to fish or hunt. We made all kinds of plans. Unfortunately, I have not seen him since boot camp. Thankfully, his name is not on The Wall. Maybe someday I will see him again. I hope and pray he made it back home alive.

My training was long and hard, but I managed to successfully survive. I had a thirty day leave before I headed to Vietnam. I tried to catch a flight from San Diego back to Ohio, but there were so many people leaving I could not get booked. So a good friend of mine got tickets for us on the train. We rode the San Francisco Chief all the way across this country. It was such a beautiful trip and it brought with it such an incredible adventure.

My buddy and I were sitting in the lounge car having a drink when the bartender all of a sudden took our drinks off the bar and put them down underneath where they could not be seen. I looked at him and said, "What are you doing?" He explained, "We are now traveling through a dry county and there are men on this train who will watch to see if we are serving liquor. If we are caught, the railroad faces a big fine, and I can lose my job." I found it hard to believe, but later learned it was indeed true.

I thoroughly enjoyed the trip, but my mother and father were unhappy because it took me such a long time to get back home. We rode the train all the way to Chicago then caught another one into

Cincinnati. When I got off the train, I looked like I had been wrung out to dry. I enjoyed the trip but was glad to be home.

My family and friends threw a party for me. It was near Christmas time and I would be leaving shortly thereafter. Those days went by so fast. When the day finally came for me to go, my family took me to the airport. It was a very hard day because everyone knew I was headed to Vietnam. Deep down they wondered if I would ever make it back and I wondered the exact same thing.

When I arrived back in California I immediately headed to staging. This is where we got our battle gear and instructions about what to expect. This was an immensely hard time. Tears would well up in my eyes as I thought about my family. I really missed them.

From there we were transported to Hawaii for a brief stop to refuel. While the plane was serviced, we were allowed to go into the terminal. It was absolutely beautiful. I had never been to Hawaii and it was certainly picturesque. As we stood in formation I watched the people as they walked by. They looked at us with disdain and treated us with little or no respect. It was as if everyone looked down their noses at us. A spark of hatred began at that very moment. Little did I realize how colossal it would become.

When we left Hawaii, we flew to Okinawa, Japan where we remained on twenty-four hour alert. For the most part we just hung out and shot pool. We generally tried to relax, but the day came when they split us up. We were all headed to Vietnam.

My first stop was Phu Bai. When we arrived, we immediately boarded a truck which transported us twenty miles down to Phu Loc. I was standing on the back of the truck manning an M60 as we raced down a dusty little road. The guys driving, clipped the bottom of a tree limb which tore off when struck. It almost took me out as well. Here I had been in Vietnam only a few hours and my own guys were trying to get me killed. We all laughed about it later. They jokingly said, "Well we had to break in the new guy."

Once we arrived in Phu Loc, I was placed in outfit Bravo One Five. At the base, I was instructed to place my sea bag in the tent with all the others. It would be the last time I saw my personal belongings, because a week later, a mortar hit our base and destroyed everything in the tent. We were no longer playing war in the woods back home. I was now in a real war in a real jungle more than seven thousand miles away from home.

Nightfall soon came and I would be immediately heading out with my outfit to an area where we planned an ambush. Normally they gave you a few nights to get acclimated to your surroundings, but this was not the case for me. They needed a machine gunner and I was chosen for the task.

As a youngster, I was used to walking through the woods at night. Back home we would always go raccoon hunting or coon huntin' as we called it. The darkness in this part of the world was nothing like I had ever experienced. It was so dark you could practically feel it. I kept reaching out and touching the guy in front of me just to make sure I had not gotten separated from the group.

Shortly thereafter, we arrived at an area alongside a small dirt road. We were instructed to dig in and get prepared. Word had it a platoon of enemy Vietnamese soldiers would be coming down this road. If that was the case, then we were to engage them.

I never dug so deep so fast in all of my life. I was determined to be as protected as possible. This was real, this was not a game. I could die. With my M60 laying in front of me and my poncho lying over my head I was vehemently praying no one would come down the road that night. Thankfully my prayers were answered. No one ever came. I was never as scared as I was that first night in Vietnam.

The next morning we got up and made a sweep of the area through some rice patty fields. One of the guys found a tunnel and went down into it to investigate. Moments later I heard a scream and ran towards the tunnel. Was the enemy inside? Had they killed one of us? Those were the questions running through my mind. It turned out that neither was the case. The guy who had went down into the tunnel needed help to get out so a buddy of mine lowered down his M16 to help him up. The rifle went off and hit the guy in the tunnel right in the rear end. He was none too happy. I can laugh about it now, but hearing that scream sent chills throughout my entire body.

When we finally got back to the base I found the nearest cot and completely crashed into a deep sleep. I was physically and emotionally spent. The next morning arrived and breakfast could not come soon enough. I was famished. When I received my rations they pointed in the basic direction I was to sit. I noticed they had spread us out all over the base. When I asked why, I was informed that the week earlier, a mortar landed in the middle of the mess tent during dinner and several groups of men were killed. After hearing the news I quickly lost my appetite.

The next night I was placed in a bunker just outside the camp with the instructions to man the M60 and protect the base. I was warned not to fall asleep or someone would sneak up behind me and slit my throat. The heavy darkness brought all kinds of sounds which made me very jumpy. It is a wonder I did not shoot myself.

I met a guy in the bunker beside me who turned out to be from the same area I was from. I tried to strike up a conversation about home, but he didn't want to talk much. Many guys did not want to get to know you well because they did not know how long you would be alive. I guess they did not want to get close to someone only to watch them die in a fight.

I remained in Phu Loc for a couple of weeks until we got notice we would be headed to Hue. The largest military campaign by the North Vietnamese Army and the Viet Cong had just gotten under way. It was known as the Tet Offensive and we would be headed straight into the middle of it.

From Phu Loc we traveled back to Phu Bai where we stayed for a day before we were loaded onto choppers headed for Hue. I was placed aboard a chinook helicopter. The back of this unit had a door which dropped down so you could load supplies into it. Another guy and I rode on the back with the door down and our machine guns at the ready so we could provide extra protection for the chopper.

As soon as we landed in Hue we began catching fire. We were outnumbered fifteen to one. Immediately, the fight began as we traveled from street to street. Throughout the entire day, bullets were fired, shots rang out, and people died. Good people I cared about were dying. The hatred in my heart was sparked and started to burn.

When the next night came, we took up position in a ditch beside one of the main thoroughfares through the city. We were just going to lay there to wait out the night. I was positioned with my M60 at one end of the street while the other machine gunner was at the opposite end. Every other member of the unit was between us. We were the first line of defense.

Laying there in the dark was mind numbing. Every sound, every noise brought anxiety. At around one or two in the morning I heard the distinct sound of footsteps. From within the ditch I slowly raised my head. From the light of the moon I could see a patrol of North Vietnamese walking by. They were so close to me I could have reached up and grabbed their ankles. There had to be at least forty or fifty of them. I felt small pebbles from the road tumbling down onto me as they marched by.

I was torn, I did not know what to do. Should I open up on them? If I did many of our guys would certainly be killed because most of them were asleep in the ditch below the road. Yet this was the same North Vietnamese who killed some of my friends in an earlier battle. Unsure about what to do I decided to hold off. I did not know if there were more behind them. I did not want to risk getting my whole unit slaughtered.

Before long they all passed by and they never knew we were there. At least on this occasion, none of our guys would die. This was certainly a big decision for a nineteen year old to make.

Every day brought death whether on our side or theirs. The next morning we began moving from block to block fighting the enemy. You could hear the B40 rockets rip down the street, screaming as they went by. The battles were intense. I would drop the bipod down on my M60 and take out as many of the enemy as I could. After a while you no longer looked at them as people, they were just targets you needed to knock down. The toll it took on my mind was devastating.

There were days in battle when I was just numb. The smell of the smoke coming off the gun, the sounds of bombs bursting in the air, and the screams of men being killed drove you literally mad. Every battle brought so much fear, but you did what you had to do to stay alive. At times it did not seem real. I felt I was standing outside my body watching the whole event take place. Most days ended with me feeling physically and emotionally spent.

I got to spend one day back at base to rest before my sergeant told me to get aboard the medevac truck. My mission was to provide security for the guys who rounded up the wounded and the dead. I immediately felt sick to my stomach. I was not prepared for what I was about to experience.

I placed my M60 on the top of the cab of the truck as we pulled out. We made our way up and down the streets looking for bodies. There were two guys in the front driving and two guys in the back with me. The guys in the back would jump off and put the bodies up on the truck. I would stay aboard and watch for enemy fire.

During a stop one of the guys yelled to me, "Hey Rickard, I need help with this one." I made my way to the back of the truck and reached down over the side to grab the flak jacket. When I pulled the guy up I saw a horrific sight. This poor man was just a body, his head and right arm had been torn completely off by enemy fire. When I got his body into the back of the truck, parts of his insides began to spew all over the floor.

My heart began to break as tears welled up in my eyes. This was somebody's son. He had no dog tags and no way for us to identify him. The only thing I knew about him was that he was an American. I swallowed hard to keep from vomiting. The whole situation made me sick and it made me infuriated.

At the next stop another body was tossed aboard and this was someone I knew. A friend I drank coffee with the day before was now lying dead at my feet. A fury of rage swelled in my heart as I shouted inside myself, *"We would not be here if these animals were not slaughtering each other."* The hatred for an entire race of people was growing greater every day.

We made several stops along the way picking up more of our dead. When we finally got back to the base I immediately went to the sergeant and told him I could not do that again. "Please just put me back with my outfit," I pleaded. He graciously complied.

The next day my unit and I made our way back into battle. Once again we went block by block engaging the enemy. At night they set me up on the front porch of a building with the instructions that anyone who came by was the enemy. In the distance I could hear what sounded like a cart coming down the road. As I positioned my weapon to fire I heard the sound of children. A Vietnamese woman was pushing a cart with a baby on top of it and two small children by her side. I let her pass only to see her killed shortly thereafter.

These communist bastards had no respect for life; not for their people, and certainly not for us. They would wire their own children with grenades and send them into the midst of us knowing dang well we would have to shoot the child to keep from being killed. These people did not deserve to live. They were a wicked vile race of people. Did they not value life?

Every day brought tragedy. We were moving along a street which had a small hill behind us when a North Vietnamese soldier snuck up from behind and fired a B40 rocket. It hit a guy just a few feet from me in the back but it did not detonate. It just passed right through him leaving a one foot diameter hole in him. You could literally see through him. Another friend killed and my hatred grew stronger.

The next day the battles got worse. We were standing in an old building when we heard a B40 rocket screaming down the street toward us. It came through the window of the building and exploded right beside me. I was thrown back against the wall and knocked almost senseless.

As I got up off the floor preparing to fire my weapon I could not find my right arm. It was somehow slung behind me. I could not feel it. I immediately ran into the next room where the corpsman was. When I stopped, my arm slung forward to the front of me so I grabbed it with my left hand.

The shrapnel from the rocket had shattered the radial and humorous bone in my right arm and severed several nerves. I was very fortunate it had not taken off my head. Immediately the corpsman laid me down on the floor and began to go to work.

It only took him a moment to realize I had a very bad injury. He turned to me and said, "Brother you have a million dollar wound." I said, "What does that mean?" He answered, "You are going home." He reached down, took out a needle and proceeded to give me two shots of morphine. I don't remember much after that.

Even though I was in bad shape, we were still under heavy fire so I could not be moved. It was a day later before they could get a jeep into where we were so I could be taken out. I was transported back to our base of operations where they had a M.A.S.H tent set up.

They put me out so they could work on my arm. When I awoke I was completely bandaged from my wrist to my shoulder. I remained there one more day before they got a chinook into the region. They loaded me and several other guys into the back and flew us to the airport. From there we were put aboard a plane and flown to Japan, then onto Alaska for refueling with our final stop being St. Louis Missouri.

When we arrived in St. Louis I was transported to the hospital. After I got placed in a room, they brought in a phone and I was allowed to call home. Everyone was at my mom and dad's house because it was my sister's birthday.

I picked up the phone, dialed the number, and waited for someone to answer. Within seconds I heard my dad say, "Hello." He was so surprised to hear my voice. With a hint of concern he asked me why I was calling and what was going on? I tried to sound nonchalant when I told him I got wounded in the arm. I could hear my father quiet the folks in the background before he asked me how bad I was. I tried to convince him I was not that bad, but my father was not buying any of it. He immediately stated, "The heck you ain't, I have been in war and I know they don't send you home for a small wound. Did they blow off your arm?" I laughed and said, "No Dad, they did not blow off my arm."

I was only in St. Louis for a day before they transported me to Great Lakes Naval Hospital in Chicago. I did not know it at the time, but I would spend a year at this facility. My arm was in really bad shape.

Originally, the doctor wanted to remove my arm and I told him no. He said, "Well, one of these days it is going to affect your back because that arm is going to feel like a lead weight you are carrying around everywhere." I said emphatically, "I don't care, you are not taking my arm!"

Over the course of the year I was there I went through numerous surgeries. Tendon transfers and bone grafts were becoming a common thing. I was surrounded by a sea of beds on both sides of the room. Rows of forty beds filled with men all injured in Vietnam. One poor guy in the corner lost his hands, legs, and was blinded. He just laid there and cried. My heart broke for him.

In my own world, I learned to dread the days they had to change the dressing on my arm. The blood would clot onto the bandages and when they pulled them off I would just sweat and scream. It was miserable. I felt like I would pass out. Once they had the dressing off, the nurses would clean the wound then reapply new bandages.

Living in a hospital brought new experiences every day and most of them were not good. When new guys arrived from Vietnam I always asked if they knew anything about my outfit back in Hue City. Most of the time they did not know anything, but on one occasion the answer was different.

They placed a soldier in the bed beside me who had several wounds, but he was in good spirits. I struck up a conversation and after a while I asked him, "Hey buddy, have you heard anything about unit Bravo One Five." He thought for a moment and said, "Yeah, I know about them. When they left Hue city the entire unit was wiped out in an ambush. Not a one survived."

Everything went black around me. I could not believe his words. I was utterly devastated. The hatred which had begun earlier was now eclipsed by what I felt in my heart. The Vietnamese people were public enemy number one. I never wanted to see another one again as long as I lived. I could care less what happened to them. In my mind, anyone who was even oriental was in the same group. I easily justified my feelings because everyone I fought with and cared about in my unit was gone.

Of course, I had no way of knowing if this guy knew about what he was talking, but it was real to me at the time. All I could think was how my friends were all gone. Hatred ruled supreme and it would for a very long time.

★ ★ ★

My parents finally made their way to Great Lakes Naval Hospital to see me. It was the first time for them to see my face since I left for Vietnam. When my mom walked into the hospital room, I was sitting on the side of the bed smoking a cigarette. Well, you know how moms are; she immediately began to lecture me about the dangers of smoking. She had completely forgotten I had been severely injured in a war. My dad spoke up and said, "Leave the boy alone he has been in a war he can smoke if he wants." The irony of the situation is still absolutely hilarious to me.

Things in the hospital were not all bad. There were people who genuinely cared about those of us who had been wounded in Vietnam. I can remember a bunch of us guys who were transported via a bus to downtown Chicago. They shut down a section of street for a block party. We ate food and music was played. It was a really nice time.

On another occasion, celebrity actress and singer, Martha Raye, had us brought to the theatre to see her star in the show *Good Time Charlie*. We were all lined up in the front row and when the play was done she came down to hug every one of us. I loved that woman; I cried the day I heard she died.

After more than a year at Great Lakes I finally got to go home. I had to check in at the VA hospital regularly, but was told my arm would never get any better. This would certainly be a nuisance because I had been right handed and I would have to learn to do everything with my left.

The life I had then was tough for me. I was consumed with hate and bitterness. I spent my time drinking my money away. I was letting my life go astray and I honestly did not care.

I was in a bar one night when my little brother came in to get me. Before we could leave, another guy began to get rowdy and called my brother outside. I was not about to let him go out alone so I followed. When we stepped out of the bar, the man pointed a gun at my brother and said, "I am going to shoot you." I immediately stepped between them and told the guy, "You are not going to kill my brother, I just got back from Vietnam and I am not about to let anything happen to him."

The situation was growing tense as the man looked me over. Angrily he pointed the gun in my face. I did not care; I just stared back and said, "You don't have the guts to pull the trigger." He just looked at me and replied, "Man you are crazy." I said, "No I am not crazy, but you are not going to shoot my brother. You will have to kill me first." He looked me over closely then put the gun away and went back inside.

A week later the same guy was buying us drinks. He became a good friend. Even had the guy pulled the trigger that night I would not have cared. I did not care about anything back then. I was so consumed with hate and bitterness, nothing in life mattered.

My mother was quite concerned for my well-being. She figured I needed someone in my life, so she introduced me to a girl she met down where she worked. Almost immediately, life began to get better. We dated for a little while before getting married in 1971. She had a young son who was three. His father wanted nothing to do with him, so I adopted the boy. He became my son.

With a family I now had a reason to live. I took my GI Bill and went to welding school. With my education complete, I went to the local steel mill to apply for a job. The doctor at the facility said "I can't approve you for the position; you have only one good arm." I said to the guy, "All I need is a chance." The doctor said, "I am sorry I can't approve you."

I was distraught, what was I going to do. I had a family to take care of and I needed a job. Luckily, my wife's mother played golf with a guy who was the head of the pipe division of the steel company. He told her, "Well send him over to me I will give him a chance." So I went for an interview and he hired me.

My job was to crawl into these pipes and grind down the drips that would occur when they were welded. I always managed to work it out some way with my arm where I could do the job. I worked there for about three months when he told me I was doing a fabulous job, but he was going to have to lay me off. Business had declined.

That was a tough blow. I was off for almost a year before I got called back. During that time I did anything I could to earn money. I painted houses both inside and out. It did not matter the job. I was willing to work to support my family.

When I was called back, they told me the only place they had for me was in the tubing division. This was the worst place to be, but I told them I would take it. I had to have a job and it did not matter to me what I did. I ended up spending nine years there and held several different positions.

During that time my wife began going to a church not far from where we lived. She began to pressure me about going with her and the kids. I worked swing shifts so I didn't always have the days off to go with her, but on one particular Sunday, I would not be working.

When Sunday came I was lying in bed half asleep. My wife came over to me and said, "Are you going to get up and go with us?" Half disgusted I mumbled, "Yes I will go." I did not want to, but I did.

Why is it when you don't want to go to church, the people you are with make you sit up near the front? Well, on this Sunday we sat in the third row and before long it felt like I was the only one in the building. A battle began to take place in my mind. I knew I needed the forgiveness he was preaching, but I knew I had been a pretty rough individual. Forgiveness certainly didn't apply to a person like me.

I was also wrestling with my hatred of the Vietnamese people. In fact, I couldn't even stand to be in the room with anyone of oriental descent. The battle grew more intense when the choir began to sing, *There is Room at the Cross for You*. The preacher looked right at me and whispered, "There is room for you." I broke down and walked the aisle to see the man who had the answers. My life was no longer mine, it belonged to Christ.

I went back to the church Sunday night and was baptized. In fact, anytime I was not at work on a Sunday I was in attendance for the services. I began to tell everyone what had transpired in my life. People noticed the difference. I was once a hell-raiser and now I was a brand new person. There was one big problem however; I still violently hated the Vietnamese.

An intense struggle was going on inside my heart and mind. I knew I received forgiveness, but the hatred still continued to grow in my soul. I could not rid my mind of the fruitless deaths of the many I cared for in Vietnam. The bitterness grew and before long it began to affect my life. I started a journey away from God.

Things were becoming so bad I could not stand to hear anyone with an oriental accent. My wife really enjoyed Chinese food, but I could not go into a restaurant because I would become so enraged at the sight of anyone who was oriental. I could not even tolerate hearing them speak through the loud speaker at a drive through window.

I tried to make my way back to the Lord several times. Of course, God accepted me with open arms, but I am sure He saw my half-hearted effort. I was just going through the motions. Sure, I was telling guys at work about how they needed Him, but it was different then. The hatred in my heart was overwhelming the love God expressed to me.

My wife saw the turmoil in my life, so she suggested I go to the VA Hospital and speak to the counselor they had on staff. She was sure they could help me. I of course, balked at the idea. She said to me, "I believe you have PTSD." I snapped back, "I don't even know what that is."

The counselor from the hospital eventually called me. I was sitting by my stove as I picked up the phone. We talked for quite some time before I broke down in tears. She said, "You really need to come here and talk with me." I finally agreed to go.

I had been dealing with this demon of hatred since 1968. It was now early in the year 2001. For thirty-three years I suffered. Even little things drove me crazy. I can remember when my sons were little, buying them a Big Wheel for Christmas. It was a toy children rode that had two wheels in the back and one large plastic wheel in the front. Those boys would get on that thing and ride up and down the street. It seemed innocent enough, but for me it was a big problem. The sound the front wheel made on the road sounded exactly like the cart the Vietnamese lady pushed the night I saw her killed. I could not tolerate it. I took the Big Wheel away from them and threw it in the garbage. The sound was torturing me.

Once I arrived at the VA and spoke to the counselor, she immediately kept me in house at the hospital for a little over three months. I went through several psychological tests and evaluations. She explained to me how even small things could trigger a flashback to something from the war. It made me realize how many times I took things out on my boys unfairly. I didn't realize it then, but I do now.

The time spent there did me good. I was still dealing with the hatred, but I seemed to have some control over it. Things at work returned to normal except for a new issue. My back was beginning to cause me severe problems. The words from the doctor at Great Lakes Naval Hospital were coming back to haunt me, "That arm is going to be like carrying around lead, it is dead weight and it will cause you back problems one day." Well, that day had arrived so I decided the best thing for me to do would be to retire from the plant.

I guess everyone will always remember where they were or what they were doing on September 11th, 2001. I was behind my house with my brother working on a boat when we got the news and saw the images of those cowards killing innocent people. The hatred returned in full force. It was just hiding inside me waiting to spring forth. I wanted to go join the military all over again. I could not stand the thought of innocent Americans being killed. I was upset and rightly so, but the hatred I had was not healthy. It was killing me ever so slowly. The Vietnamese had not succeeded in killing me, but the hatred I had for them was doing so.

The next year things got undeniably bad with my back. I was in very poor condition. After going to the doctor it was determined I was going to need surgery. I was scheduled a few days later to go under the knife. My good friend Sam, along with my entire family escorted me to the hospital. I was in surgery for more than thirteen hours. Everyone enduringly sat around in the waiting room anxious for any shred of news about my condition.

The surgeons cut me down the middle of my stomach and went through into my back. Next they rolled me over and cut me down the back as well. It was as if they carved me in half. Once I came out of surgery they put me in the recovery room.

However, I was not recovering, I was struggling. My oxygen levels were dropping and my blood pressure was extremely low. My wife, who was a nurse, knew the gravity of the situation. She sat in the room waiting for me to open my eyes.

When I finally came to I asked her how everything was going and she looked at me with a very worried expression and told me it did not look good. I did not understand what she meant, so I asked her point blank, "What do you mean it does not look good?" With a tear running down her cheek she looked me in the eyes and said, "Honey you are dying. I do not know if you are going to get out of here."

My whole body was just shutting down. The strain of surgery had taken its toll. They tried to get me to eat but I just threw it right back up. Knowing the desperation of the situation my wife escorted everyone out of the room. As I laid there alone I thought about death. It seemed like an eternity passed before she returned.

When my wife walked back into the room she said, "I just spoke to a doctor here who says she can save you." I said, "Well where is she?" My wife replied, "She is right outside the door in the hallway." I anxiously answered, "Well why hasn't she come in?" My wife looked at me very intently and said, "Because she is Vietnamese."

Her words hit me like a ton of bricks. Here I am lying in a hospital with my body shutting down; nearing the point of death and the only doctor who can help me is Vietnamese. In my heart I knew God placed me in this situation to force me to deal with my hatred once and for all. I could go on hating a whole race of people because of something a few did in Vietnam and die, or I could let it go and live.

I looked at my wife and said, "What did you say?" She replied, "She is Vietnamese and she will not come in here unless you ask her. I told her about how you feel about Vietnamese people so she will not come in unless you say it is okay." I disgustingly replied, "Is there not anyone else in the whole hospital who can help me?" My wife said, "No there is not and we do not have time to look for anyone else. Honey, she can save your life, please let her try."

Decision time had come. What was it going to be? I could not wait around any longer. I was told I would not live out the night if something was not done soon. My situation was getting drastically worse. At that moment I had to give all the anger I had for the Vietnamese people to God. When I turned my life over to Jesus I kept back this area and now God was forcing me to deal with it. I decided it was time to give Him my all. I told my wife to send her in.

A flood of emotion came over me as she stepped into the room and walked over to my bed. She softly patted me on the arm and quietly asked where I served in Vietnam. When I told her the numerous cities, she replied, she never visited those places because it was much too dangerous.

She explained to me how she was a pediatrician in Vietnam and how the Viet Cong did appalling things to her. She also shared how her and her husband escaped the country by boat. She was one of the original Vietnamese boat people who fled the country. Once she got to America she continued her education and now she was the head of the entire Intensive Care Unit at the hospital.

I thought to myself how ironic the situation was because I could remember how angry I got when I heard about these Vietnamese boat people coming to America. Now my life was in the hands of one of them.

She talked to me for a short while to put my mind at ease. She said confidently, "I can help you." Within minutes she gave the nurses orders to bring the instruments she needed. When they arrived she took a scalpel and placed it gently against my neck. Immediately I thought, *Here I lay about to let a Vietnamese woman cut my throat with a knife when thousands of Vietnamese men tried unsuccessfully to do it years earlier.*

She took the scalpel and made a small incision in my neck where they placed a tube to give me shots and injections. I was placed in the Intensive Care Unit where I remained for the next three weeks. During the entire time she worked diligently making sure I was getting the best care. Her treatment was an overwhelming success. She literally saved my life.

My last night in ICU, I laid in my bed and begged God to forgive me for hating people I never met or knew existed. I wept because of the hatred I had for so long for an entire race of people. I judged them all for the wrong doing of a few. Immediately, the weight and burden of this horrible sin was lifted. My demon was gone. The people I once hated became my healer. It was an amazing transformation.

The three weeks I was in ICU that Vietnamese doctor came in everyday to talk with me. She showed genuine compassion and concern. In fact, she is still my doctor to this very day. She is a person I am proud to call my friend. I am amazed and in awe at how God used the very people I declared were my enemy to save my life.

There are times now when I need a place to retreat; a place where my mind can find peace from the daily turmoil life can bring. For me it is the memory of a small farm where I lived when I was five-years-old. It was a beautiful sunny Sunday morning. My mother took me, my older sister, and my younger brother to church on that warm summer day. As we walked along the road I could smell the honeysuckle bush wrapped around the fence post. Butterflies floated in the air with not a care in the world. The quarter of mile walk to the church seemed to take no time at all. Everything in my world was perfect.

It was a small, white, one room church building with hardwood floors throughout. I remember holding my mother's hand as I made my way carefully up the stairs. The room full of wooden pews and a small pulpit at the front bore a glorious message to all who would enter. My mother's angelic voice sung the sweet hymns of the Lord to all who were in attendance.

At the end of the service we walked home and us kids changed into our play clothes while my mother prepared lunch. She took all of us out through the back door into the field behind our home. She brought along a picnic lunch she prepared. As we ran and played, my mind was carefree and innocent. No hate, no killing, and no bitterness. This was the way life was meant to be.

My mother is gone now, but the memory of that day still lives on. Her warm smile and loving care were so evident to me. She loved us unconditionally. I didn't know it then, but I now know what she wanted us to see. On that summer Sunday morning she was trying to introduce us to the God of forgiveness, peace, and LIBERTY.

Gave Proof through the Night

As my wife and I sat in the conference room, the lights shining down from the ceiling became very dim. I could hear voices in the room yet I could see no faces. The whole building appeared to spin as if I was experiencing a late night episode of the *Twilight Zone*. Cold sweat ran down my neck as my heart raced within my chest. Seconds later, my mind came crashing back to reality as the doctor cleared his voice and said, "Sir, did you hear what I said to you? Your son is dead, there is nothing we can do." I could not believe their words, I would not believe their words. My name is Billy and this is my story.

I remember the day I learned I was going to be a father. Excitement, joy, fear, and anticipation ran through my soul like an unbridled thoroughbred in a pasture. However, waiting for the day to arrive compared more to the movement of a snail. The long months of expectation finally reached their happy conclusion when the doctor handed me my new bundle of joy and said, "Billy, you have got yourself a healthy baby boy." Neither of us knew at the time just how wrong his words would be.

It was true I did have a new son and I was certainly thankful for such a precious gift. I was determined, like most fathers, to do my best to raise an honest, hardworking boy.

For me, getting married at a young age was never much of an issue, but soon after Kalan arrived, the stress and strain began to pull on both of us. Unfortunately, it pulled my wife and me apart, resulting in the dissolution of our marriage.

It is truly a tragedy when a father can only be with his son part-time because of the breakup of the family, but I was determined to make sure Kalan knew he had a father who loved him very much. I made a commitment to him and I stuck to it.

Amidst all the difficulty and trials, everything managed to work out. Through the years my son, Kalan, became the kind of boy I always wanted. He was fun-loving, good natured, and all boy. He knew how to rough house, play sports, and most important to me, he knew how to fish. He was just the kind of son every man wants when he bows his head and prays to God for a baby boy.

Kalan was a good kid. Oh, he had his ups and downs like most boys growing up, but watching him slowly develop into a young man was exciting for me. Not only was he strong, he was athletic. Football became his passion and folks around town soon took notice of his gridiron abilities.

When Kalan began high school, he immediately made an impact in his new school. With an electric personality along with athletic skills that make coaches drool, he quickly became the big man on campus. It was clearly noted by all that Kalan was his name and football was his game.

His freshman year was normal for the most part, with success coming both on the field and in the classroom. However, when his sophomore year started things began to take an ominous turn. It started out as something very small, but in the end it meant the battle for whether Kalan lived or died.

Football is a very rough game, both physically and mentally. Those things did not matter to Kalan, he was determined to be the very best athlete he could. The practices were long and hard, but the results on the field echoed the dividends. Kalan dealt with the bumps and bruises well. Even though he played both running back and linebacker, he never had any trouble dealing with the soreness that came from playing such a physically demanding sport. He managed to take every hurt in stride. Yet, there was one issue constantly nagging him; a pain in his chest.

The pain was something his mother and I never knew anything about. Kalan kept it to himself. I guess maybe he thought it was a part of the game of football, but when the season was long over the pain remained.

His junior year of high school came and went just like the previous year. He was better than ever on the field, but the pain in his chest was still there; ever so slowly getting worse. By the time his senior year arrived Kalan dominated the gridiron while the chest pain grew to dominate his life.

Kalan went on to graduate from high school and because of family responsibilities he bypassed college and got a job with a local landscape company installing sprinkler systems. Life would certainly be different in the working world, but Kalan did not care.

He was at his new job for only two weeks when his chest felt like it was going to explode. When the pains started years earlier he thought nothing of it, but it could no longer be ignored. The pain was so great, he called his girlfriend Kellie and let her know what was going on. Thankfully she made an appointment for Kalan with his family doctor.

The next morning, they went to the doctor. It was a typical visit; information forms were completed, vital signs were checked, and his height and weight were measured. Everything, including his blood pressure and pulse, all showed as normal.

Moments later the doctor made his way into the room to begin the examination. Questions were asked and everything was carefully documented. Within minutes they had the answer.

The doctor looked at Kalan and said, "What you are experiencing is nothing more than simple growing pains; nothing more, nothing less."

Wow, nothing but growing pains. I know when I spoke with Kalan about the visit he felt foolish for having mentioned the chest pains, but how was he or any of us to know it was something so simple.

Kalan went back to work the next day and continued to go about his daily routine. However, the pain was not routine. It was getting worse. There had to be something more to this.

When the pain began to take his breath, Kalan knew another trip to the doctor was in order. This time things did not go quite as smoothly. This time, the visit took a drastic turn. We are not sure if the doctor noticed something different or just felt concerned, but nevertheless he decided it was time for Kalan to see a specialist. An appointment was made and within days my boy headed to the recommended cardiologist for diagnosis.

Much like the other visits, the same things were done in the beginning. To the nurse, all his vital signs appeared to check out as normal. Kalan and Kellie waited until finally the cardiologist arrived. He asked them several questions and listened carefully to Kalan's heart rhythms. After the examination he decided Kalan needed to have an EKG or electrocardiogram test as it is also known.

The cardiologist explained to him, "This test is going to check for any problems within the electrical activity of your heart. After I get the results, I should be able to find the cause of your unexplained chest pains."

When I got the news, I was on a large construction project in Virginia. Kellie was frantic on the other end of the phone.

"Kalan has an aneurysm in the main artery in the top of his heart," she tearfully explained. "They have also discovered he was born without a valve in the lower chamber of his heart."

The news was crushing to me. How could my healthy, strong, and physically active son have a condition which could kill him? I immediately did like most folks do, I questioned myself and I questioned God. I felt like a man having so many questions and nowhere to go for answers.

I could hear over the phone Kellie was extremely upset, then she said the words that terrified me, "You need to get to Alabama immediately, there is no time to lose."

Just days before, everything in my life was ordinary and now my son was fighting for his life. In my mind, time screeched to a stop and the beating of my heart slowed to a crawl. The question racing to the forefront was this; *Would my boy live or was his time on this planet about to expire?* No one knew for certain, but I begged God to spare the life of Kalan. I only hoped He would answer my prayer.

Without a moment to spare I made my way from Virginia to Alabama. The entire trip felt like an eternity. My thoughts battled in my mind like two great armies waging war. Kellie told me on the phone they sedated Kalan and an operation would be performed on him first thing Sunday morning.

Why do we always think the worst of things will happen when something like this occurs? I wanted to believe everything would be okay, but waves of doubt crashed through my head like a tsunami slamming into the shore.

After what seemed like days, I finally arrived in Alabama. I immediately made my way to the hospital where Kalan was being treated. The white walls faded into the floor as I walked down the hallway to his room. As I slowly opened the door, I tried to show a positive face on the outside, but a negative one was hiding beneath.

Just getting to see my son meant the world to me. Even though the situation was not good, I just felt better knowing I was there with him.

After seeing Kalan, the next person I immediately wanted to see was the doctor. I had to know the specifics of what was going on.

What were my son's chances? Just how serious was his condition? A thousand more questions ran through my mind like a herd of buffalo rumbling across an open prairie.

I don't know what it is about sitting in a hospital waiting room, but time appears to move so slowly. I have often heard the old saying, "a watched pot never boils," well I believe also a watched clock in a hospital never moves. Finally, after what seemed like hours, the surgeon who would perform the operation came into the room.

He was a slender man of average height with an attitude of confidence, bordering on arrogant. At this time, it did not matter to me about his personality, all I wanted to know is could he save my son.

He approached me and calmly stated, "Mr. Cooley, your son has an aneurysm in the main artery in the top of his heart. Also, he has no valve in the lower chamber of his heart. I want you to know Mr. Cooley that I have performed sixty-three of these surgeries in my career and your son Kalan is the healthiest person I will have ever worked on. This should be nothing but routine."

As I listened to the doctor focus on the details, my mind seemed to shift away from the room as if I was on the outside looking down in. Was all of this really happening? How could my eighteen year-old former star football player son have open heart surgery? Was this all just a horrible dream?

I quickly came back to my senses when I heard an ominous warning from the surgeon. "Mr. Cooley, I want you to know, should the aneurysm burst while we are operating on your son, there will be nothing we can do. He will die on the operating table if that occurs."

There it was, the words I did not want to hear. "Your son will die." Over and over the words echoed off the wall. The sound was deafening, the room grew black and despair began to rear its ugly head. Quickly, I snapped out of those thoughts and back to the situation at hand.

The surgeon, sensing my concern turned and spoke confidently, "Once again, let me reassure you. I have done sixty-three of these surgeries. All have been a success and your son Kalan is by far the healthiest of all my patients."

My mind was torn, wrestling about in apprehension. On one hand, I was comforted at the confidence of this surgical doctor, but on the other hand there was an aura of arrogance about him that brought me great concern. Maybe I was imagining it all. Maybe he wasn't arrogant, maybe he just felt good about what he could perform. Even if this was the case, it still made me feel uneasy about the situation.

As the surgeon left the room I looked over at Kalan who laid there as if he had not a concern in the world. I don't know if he was fearless or just naïve because of his age, but he was already talking about walking out of the hospital once everything was over. Never once did it seem to cross his mind the gravity of the situation. However, I knew the weight of the matter, so I did enough worrying for the both of us.

Sunday morning, August 13th, 2005, the day arrived just like any other on the calendar. Yet today would be the day I would find out if my son lived or died. Every member of Kalan's extended family converged onto the hospital grounds. Each person sharing their love for my boy before they wheeled him back to surgery.

I did not want to let him go, but I knew he must. The pain of watching him roll away and knowing everything was out of my control was just overwhelming. The nurses reassured me time and time again that the surgeon knew what he was doing. "Sir you have nothing to fear everything will be okay." I only wished I knew for sure I could believe their words.

They wheeled Kalan back into the surgery unit where he went through the procedures that occur when you go under the knife. Vitals were taken, the anesthesia was administered, and soon, my boy was medically unconscious. The surgery began.

Outside in the waiting room the entire family was gathered. Stories were shared, concerns were aired and prayers were ushered to the gates of Heaven; every one of us hoped they would find their way inside.

I watched the clock. It did not move. Every minute seemed to take more than an hour to pass. With every tick of the second hand I was adding years to my own life. I was a father in his forties, but I felt like a man over eighty. The time just dragged on. Six hours passed and the surgery was still ongoing.

Why is it taking so long? I needed to know something. I tried asking a nurse for more information. She just reassured me everything was going as scheduled. At this point I felt like they should schedule me for surgery, because my heart was pounding on the walls of my chest trying to get free.

Eight hours, still in surgery, still no word. Nine hours, ten hours, eleven hours, and then some news. The surgery was over and the news was good. Kalan would live!

The surgeon let us know the surgery was an overwhelming success. We were told they were moving Kalan to the Cardiac Intensive Care Unit and shortly we would be able to see hm. I thanked the surgeon, but more importantly I thanked God for sparing my son.

I was really not prepared for what I would see when we walked into Kalan's room. My son was laying there with every tube you can imagine hooked to his body. I surveyed the room looking at every machine until I noticed a particular one that grabbed my attention. It was the one used to monitor Kalan's heartbeat.

My eyes were glued to every movement, every sound. Something did not seem right. His heart was beating rapidly and very hard. In fact the beat of his heart was actually causing his bed to move. Every contraction made it move slightly. It was as if I was watching the minor tremors of an earthquake happening right before my eyes.

This brought me great concern, but what I saw next had me seriously worried. Coming out of Kalan's chest was a long tube used to drain excess blood from the wound. My eyes became fixated upon it. After watching for a few minutes I was convinced Kalan was expelling a tremendous amount of blood. Certainly this could not be normal.

I quickly stepped outside my son's room and asked the nurse if she could contact the surgeon and let him know I had some questions. She gladly obliged and within a reasonable amount of time I saw the surgeon making his way down the hall.

As I approached him I noticed the look of disdain on his face. When I brought up the subject about the amount of blood coming from the tube in my son's chest you could tell he was clearly annoyed. With an expression of disgust he said, "Well some people bleed a lot. Look you just need to go back to your hotel room because you can't see him anymore tonight. He will be fine, I am the specialist here, the one with the training and credentials. I know what I am doing."

With those words of arrogance he turned and walked away. The nurse then came and we were ushered from the room. I felt angry, hurt, and insulted. This was my son and I had every right to be concerned. I was entitled to express them to the surgeon or anyone else in this hospital. I knew I should be grateful to this man who saved my son's life, but I could not get past his words or demeanor.

So I did the only thing I could do, I waited in the parking lot for the surgeon to exit the hospital, we were going to have words man to man. Well not really, that never happened, but I can say I did think about it. Reluctantly I went back to our hotel and tried to get some much needed rest. Yet sleep would not come because within the hour the hospital called to tell us they had to rush Kalan back into surgery. The reason; excessive bleeding.

Now I had a right to be mad. The arrogance or negligence of the surgeon placed my boy at risk. Without a moment to spare we were back at the hospital and into the waiting room.

One hour passed and no news. Two, three, four hours passed and nothing on the status of my son. Finally after five hours of surgery to stop the excessive bleeding we got the news Kalan would be fine.

This time the surgeon said few words to us and when I finally got to see my boy I felt more at ease than when I had before. I am no doctor and I have no medical training, but things just looked better to me now. I just knew Kalan was going to be okay. Unfortunately, that was not going to be the case.

Time seemed to return to its normal pace for the next few days and by the end of the week Kalan was strong enough to return home. I was feeling grateful to have my son out of the hospital. He acted as if nothing happened to him. He was the same normal, fun-loving boy I always knew. Things could finally get back to normal.

However, things did not get back to normal. Exactly one week after his initial surgery Kalan woke up in the night because he could not breathe. He was grabbing at his chest, gasping for air and his whole complexion was changing rapidly in front of our eyes.

Without any hesitation, my mother and father, who were staying with Kalan, contacted the hospital. They were told to get him there immediately. They wasted no time in following the instructions. As soon as he arrived at the hospital, it was clear Kalan would once again require surgery.

Family and friends converged onto the hospital campus yet again. The waiting game began. However, this time the clock never moved, in fact, I believe it ticked backward. The anxiety and despair I had before the first surgery were being multiplied a thousand times over. This certainly did not seem to bode well. The same surgical team once again had my son's life in their hands and by now my confidence in them was shaky.

Another twelve hours passed before we got any kind of news, but this time it was not good. The surgeon walked slowly into the waiting area and pulled me aside. He said, "Your son is in grave condition, we had some complications occur during the procedure and right now all we can do is wait."

Before I could say anything he boldly stated, "This is all I can tell you at this time." He then walked away.

The words were crushing, but the attitude in which they were delivered felt heartless. There was no compassion or concern coming from him. His words were being spewed like random facts coming from a machine placed in a corner.

I was both furious and heartbroken at the same time. I had no clue what to do, where to go or how to act. My whole world seemed to be spinning out of control. This was my son, my flesh and blood; this was not just some random statistic or blob of flesh in there. I felt so useless. All I could do was sit around and wait. Damn, how I hate clocks!

Kalan managed to live through that Sunday night and we made our way back to the hospital Monday morning. They allowed us to see Kalan, but only for fifteen minutes at a time and only four times the entire day. As slow as time moved in the waiting room, it sped by like a NASCAR driver at Daytona when we were by Kalan's side.

Monday came and went with no word from anyone on the condition of my son. Tuesday came and our entire existence revolved around the hospital waiting area. We hoped for any word or sign of encouragement from anyone about Kalan. We got nothing.

On Wednesday I reached my breaking point. I needed to talk to someone. I demanded to know what was going on. I was clearly upset and the nurse took us down to the hospital administrator. She took us into her office and said, "Mr. Cooley, I need you to meet us here tomorrow morning at 10:00am. We can then explain everything to you."

Well it was news, but their answer brought even more questions. What were they going to say? Why did it have to wait until tomorrow? What is going on with my son? Needless to say I got no sleep that night. The clock taunted me all evening long, mocking my very existence and dependence on its abilities.

Thankfully, Thursday morning did come even though the clock tried to prevent it from ever happening. Maybe deep down it knew what was coming. After getting dressed, we drove to the hospital, then walked the short distance to the conference area.

As we entered the room I could see seated around the long board room table was the hospital administrator, the cardiac care physician, a neurologist, the heart surgeon, and the hospital chaplain. They all sat flanked on one side of the table and we were positioned directly across from them.

The surgeon coldly began to explain why we were here. "On Sunday during surgery a blood clot formed in the chamber of Kalan's heart where we placed the St Jude's valve. Because of this clot your son died during surgery and was dead for forty minutes. During this time we massaged his heart and managed to resuscitate it. However, we cannot specifically tell you the oxygen levels available to his brain during this time but we do know brain damage did occur. While we were massaging his heart the blood clot in that chamber went through his heart up to the brain causing him to have a stroke on both sides. This has resulted in your son being brain dead."

The neurologist picked up Kalan's brain scan and showed it to us. "As you can see here this is the brain scan of your son and I have here a comparison of a brain scan of someone who is living. The results clearly show your son, for all intents and purposes, is dead. He will never regain consciousness. His brain waves have the same consistency as a bowl of Jell-O. In fact, I can get more brain activity out of a bowl of Jell-O than I can out of your son. His heart is beating, but that is just because we are making it happen, other than that he is dead."

No, I could not believe it. I would not believe it. This could not be happening. How could my son be dead? How could they let this happen? Why would God let this happen? So many questions and so few answers. Everything I ever knew just blew up in front of my eyes.

The administrator now turned and told us, "You now need to make your peace with Kalan and think about what is best for him.

You cannot focus on your feelings you need to make the arrangements to let him go."

This was the final straw, I was furious. It was my turn to say something. I looked across the long cold table and boldly declared to them, "If it is not within your power or capacity to fix him, then you need to tell us where we need to take him, because that is what we are going to do. Because, him not walking out of here is not an option! My son walked in here and he is going to walk out."

I became very visibly upset and pointed at the surgeon, "You are the reason my son is in this condition. You bragged about your sixty-three other surgeries and how Kalan was the healthiest person you every worked on. Stating how this would be nothing but a walk in the park. Your arrogance sir, has killed my son!"

I wanted to climb across the table and mop up the floor with him, but I managed to keep my composure. The thing so aggravating was just the callousness of the entire group. It felt so heartless and cold.

I looked them all squarely in the eyes and stated, "I will not let you kill my son, he will walk out of this hospital. You can take that to the bank." We walked out of the conference room and down the hall to the Cardiac Intensive Care Unit. I walked over to my son reached down to his face and began to talk to him like I did every time we were together. I was not about to let him go, but the hospital had a different plan and I was prepared to fight them every step of the way.

Over the course of the next five weeks I spent every moment I was allowed in that room with my son. We could visit him fifteen minutes four times a day. One hour, one stinking hour was all I got with my boy each day, but I was determined to take advantage of the time I had with him.

While all of this was going on something else interesting was happening. People from all over the country began to pray for my son. I traveled quite a bit during my life, doing construction jobs all over the United States. Once word got out about what was trans-piring with Kalan, people began to call, telling me how they were praying for him. I was reassured by so many that God would give proof through the darkest of nights He would be there for Kalan.

Throughout this entire ordeal I had no clue what was happen-ing, but for the first time I began to wonder, "Is there something else going on here?" Only time would tell what the answer would be. Right now however, I had more than enough questions.

Each time I went in to be with Kalan I treated him the same way I did when he was conscious. I played music, told jokes, and shared normal stories about my day. On more than one occasion, I leaned down to tell Kalan a joke and would begin laughing before I could ever get the punch line out. I am sure people walking by thought I was crazy, but I knew my son was alive. I knew he was not dead. I did not care what a brain scan or some arrogant surgeon had to say. I knew the truth. Kalan was alive and he would walk out of this hospital.

I would like to say I was confident all the time, but to be perfectly honest, most of it was probably denial. I did not want to believe what was happening. I did not want to think my son could be dead. I figured if I denied this was happening then it would cease to be true.

Also during this time I was bargaining with God. You all know how it goes. Hey God, if you spare him this is what I will do. We have all done it and in my mind I can imagine how funny it must seem to the Creator to see such frail human beings trying to make a deal. I was hoping things were going to get better, but unfortunately they got worse.

There is an old saying that states, "It is always darkest before the dawn." I soon learned how true these words were when Hurricane Katrina slammed into New Orleans and the Gulf Coast of Missis-sippi. People everywhere lost their homes and many folk lost their lives. The hurricane was devastating for my extended family because most everyone lived on or near the locations hardest hit. Not only were we losing our son, my family members were losing their homes and livelihoods. Darkness was ruling the day.

Yet, during this time while sitting at the hospital watching the news about the destruction, my father looked over to me and said, "If the only problems we have in this world is that we lost our home then we really don't have any problems now do we?" I was amazed at the statement and turned and said, "No, I guess we don't."

Throughout this entire five week period I was amazed at what I was seeing occur in my family and within myself. My sister kept reassuring me Kalan would be ok. She always believed he would live. I wanted to believe it as well, but I have to admit I was beginning to have my doubts.

Through the midst of all this, there were things happening I could not explain. We had a little apartment near the hospital where we were staying so we could be close to Kalan every day. On one occasion, my wife went to the laundry mat to wash our clothes. While she was there her cell phone rang and a woman from Hawaii was on the other end. Within a few moments, my wife knew this woman had the wrong number. However, before she could end the call the woman said, "I really feel like you are under a tremendous weight of stress and strain. You have something terrible troubling you I just know it, but I want you to know that everything is going to be ok." My wife just broke down. Over the course of the next hour and a half this total stranger prayed and talked to my wife about the situation. To this very day we look back in amazement of how a wrong number turned into such a blessing.

All the wonderful support I received from family and friends was being counteracted by the constant barrage of advice from the hospital staff. Each day we were being told, "Mr. Cooley you need to turn off the life support. You have to accept that your son is dead, there is nothing anyone can do to change the fact." This was something I was not willing to believe.

On the very first morning after that five week period I walked into Kalan's room just like I always did and leaned down to tell him my latest joke. However this time something different happened; Kalan grinned. Immediately I shot out of the room exclaiming, "My son just grinned, come quick my son just grinned."

We were all hopeful and very enthusiastic, but the hospital staff basically did not believe what I was telling them. In fact, the neurologist told me it was just nerves from his primal reflexes. I looked at him and said, "What are primal reflexes?" I was soon instructed those are reflexes we have because we have evolved. I turned and said, "Maybe you evolved, but I was created and my boy is in there and he can hear me."

To this day I never understood why they were so anxious to pull the plug on my boy. I was in an institution founded to save people's lives and they were hell-bent on ending Kalan's. I was determined to make sure that did not happen.

Over the next two weeks I saw the beginnings of a miracle. One day, while I was in the room telling him a joke, he opened his eyes and smiled. It was the first time I saw his eyes open since before the surgery. I could tell he was in there but communication was a problem.

Even though these things were occurring the hospital staff still was in denial of what was taking place. So, I then found a way Kalan could communicate with me. I said, "Kalan if you would like a drink of water blink your eyes twice." Kalan immediately blinked twice. Over and over again I would ask him a question and he would answer with a blink. After two weeks of that the staff had to agree Kalan was in there. He really could hear us. Just like I always stated, 'Kalan is alive!" The darkness left because the dawn arrived.

Yes, it was true my son was alive, but he was also blind. The effects of the two strokes on his brain, as well as the blood clot rendered his vision non-existent. Nevertheless we knew we were witnessing a miracle and we were not about to discount what had just taken place.

My eighteen year old son, who was dead on the operating table, who the doctors stated had no brain activity, and should be unplugged then buried in the ground was alive. He was a living, breathing, and communicating human being who deserved a chance at life. I was going to make sure he got every opportunity to return to normal. If that was going to happen, I knew I had to get Kalan out of this ward of death before anything else could go wrong.

Within days, Kalan left the hospital and it was a day of triumph. Although he was not well, he was alive, and we were determined to ensure he got the best treatment possible. I just could not let him stay in a place where they were constantly trying to get us to end his life. I had no trust they would do the right thing for him.

After doing some research we chose a very reputable rehabilitation facility in Alabama. In fact they are considered one of the best in the entire nation. I knew this would be the place where my son could get better.

When we arrived at the facility we were immediately greeted by the therapists and counselors who would be responsible for Kalan's rehabilitation. We spoke for quite some time before they gave us their assessment.

One of the counselors turned to me and said, "Mr. Cooley we believe if your son Kalan works hard and applies himself, then maybe someday he might be able to dress himself, but this is the best you can ever hope for."

I really did not know whether to laugh or to be angry. I had just left a hospital of people who tried to convince me to kill my son and now I was amongst a group of folks who believed he would be nothing more than just a shell of himself. Deep down I knew they were trying to be helpful, but there was a part of me that was sad for them. They were talking to a man who had already witnessed one miracle and I had full faith in God another was going to occur.

★ ★ ★

Therapy began in earnest the very first day we took Kalan to the facility. The folks were kind to him and Kalan progressed more quickly than anyone could have imagined. Not only did he begin to speak again, but his vision was slowly returning. He was still legally blind because he could only see some dots and shapes, but we felt very good about what was transpiring.

As I watched Kalan change I also realized I was changing. This fact occurred to me when I witnessed a seventy year old man brought to the facility with a broken back. The gentleman was the sole survivor in his family. Everyone else was killed by Hurricane Katrina. The gravity of his situation weighed on me heavily. I was always proud to be a rough construction worker, managing building projects all over the nation worth hundreds of millions of dollars. Who I thought I was and what I did for a living no longer mattered. The only thing that mattered now was the relationship with my son. I was determined to redeem the time we had together. Not only was Kalan getting a second chance at life, but so was I.

Even though the process of rehabilitation was difficult, it did come with things that made us laugh. We soon discovered Kalan had no concept of time. His memory was very short term. A person could walk right up to him, introduce themselves, and moments later Kalan would ask the person who they were. Then a few minutes later he would do it again.

What became so funny to all of us was watching Kalan enjoy a program on TV. He could literally watch the same exact thing over and over again laughing so hard, like he was watching it for the very first time. As I share this now it might not seem like progress, but when your son is laying in a hospital bed and they tell you he is dead, you will give anything to hear him laugh again. I was certainly getting my request.

Within about a year Kalan began to regain more of his vision. He could make out shapes and see some colors. In fact, I can remember him telling me on one occasion how he always thought a certain nurse had red hair and come to find out she was really a blonde.

Even though he could not fully see everything Kalan liked to fake it. He did not want anyone to know he needed help to do something. I remember on one occasion when we went to Red Lobster for dinner. During the course of the meal, Kalan excused himself to go the restroom. I asked if he needed help finding the place and he said, "No I can find it." After a short time my wife turned to me and said, "Kalan has been gone for quite a while maybe you should go check on him." I made my way to the back of the restaurant then down the hall to the restrooms. As I turned the corner I saw Kalan walk out of the ladies room. He had no clue he had went into the wrong place. The funny thing about the whole situation were the ladies who came out right after him. They just looked at me with a wry smile on their faces and walked on past. I just shook my head and laughed.

After more than a year in rehab Kalan's vision really began to improve, but he had no depth perception. Because of this he was still considered to be legally blind. This did not stop Kalan from trying to convince me he was ready to drive again. One day he came to me and said, "Daddy, can I drive?" I turned and asked, "Well, can you drive?" Kalan was always quick with a response so he stated, "I don't know if I can or not, no one will let me try." He had a point, so I took him down to a little subdivision near where we lived and put him behind the wheel. I soon learned the hard way he was not ready to drive. He would see a sign in the distance and because he had no depth perception he would not stop at the right place. One time it might be two feet away and the next it would be two hundred. I soon felt like I was driving around town with my great grandmother who could not see.

Even though these things were a frustration to Kalan, they were actually a blessing to me. How many fathers get a second chance in life to teach their son the things they find important. I had the opportunity to help my son become a grown man all over again.

After about two years of therapy, Kalan came again to me and said, "Daddy, when can I drive?" I told Kalan once he got his driver's license and passed the eye exam I would get him a car. So when he asked me the question I countered by asking him, "Well Kalan, can you drive?" I was not ready for the answer he gave, but it certainly had me laughing and shaking my head at the same time.

He said, "Well Daddy, when the guys and I go out some nights they all drink and you know I don't. Well, since they are too drunk to drive they make me the designated driver and I drive everyone home." I thought to myself, "Let me get this straight, the legally blind kid is the designated driver for a bunch guys who are too drunk to get home on their own." Wow, I guess truth is stranger than fiction.

Before long Kalan passed his eye exam, got his driver's license and was ready to hold down a steady job. It was about three years since that fateful day the hospital staff told me my son was dead and I needed to let him go. Now he was once again a productive member of society. Sure there were still areas in his mind not at one hundred percent, but his progress was absolutely remarkable.

The area in which he was still having the most difficulty was his concept of time. Kalan could not tell you if ten minutes or five hours had passed. I can remember giving him a job to do on a construction site down in Savannah Georgia. I assigned him to sand an area we were going to paint. The section was only about a foot and a half by two feet so I left Kalan to the task and went about my business. I got so tied up with what I was doing I forgot about Kalan. When I returned five hours later he was still working on the same spot. He had no clue it had been five hours. He thought only a few minutes had passed.

Even though Kalan was dealing with this issue, working with me on the construction sites helped him to progress greatly. He had to write things down, use his fine motor skills and build up his strength. My boy became normal again, but I would never ever be the same. I witnessed firsthand a miracle from God. It was undeniable, it really, truly happened.

More than nine years have passed since the day Kalan died in surgery. What an incredible journey it has been to watch my son transformed from a lifeless shell into a productive member of society with two beautiful daughters. The boy who was left for dead by the folks in that cardiac care unit, was now a man. I felt Kalan was ready to pay the hospital staff a visit. I wanted them to witness with their own eyes the miracle they tried to destroy.

It was a bright, beautiful, sunny day when Kalan walked back into the hospital and onto the floor of the Cardiac Intensive Care Unit. Nurses stopped in their tracks when they found out who he was. Huge drops of tears poured to the ground as they witnessed my boy alive and well in front of them.

I was especially anxious to confront the hospital administrator, the surgeon, and neurologist who told me over and over again, "Your son is brain dead. You need to do what is best for him and just pull the plug."

When Kalan stepped in front of these people they had no words to say. They could not explain what happened. They just stood there with shocked looks on their faces. There were so many things I wanted to say to them, but I suppressed them all because I did not want to make this moment about me. No, this moment belonged to God. He showed a group of folks who thought they had all the answers that they really didn't even know the questions. I told them Kalan would walk out of this hospital and on that glorious day we did it together.

As I close my story I want to say one more thing. What if the government or a hospital gains the right to overrule the wishes of the parents or guardians of a patient? What if a panel of bureaucrats somewhere can decide who should live or who should die based on some chart of statistics? If this would have been the case in 2005, then my son Kalan would not be here today. Never forget life is a precious gift from God, it is not something to be taken for granted. I pray we will always remember this fact.

During the 1980 Olympic Games the United States Hockey team defeated the Soviet Union for the gold medal. At approximately the eight second mark of the game the announcer, Al Michaels jubilantly cries out, "Do you believe in miracles? Yes!" It is a statement which has been played over and over again in the world of sports. I would like to take the opportunity now to answer the question he so passionately asked on that day. Do you believe in miracles? Yes Al Michaels, I most certainly do.

That Our Flag was Still There

The red, white, and blue striped pole whirled slowly as I walked by. Never before had I heard it speak, but today would be different. Today it spoke loud and clear. I was mesmerized as I stopped and stared at the bright shiny object slowly turning in front of my eyes. The light blazing through its glorious stripes exclaimed one story after another until a sudden terrible wind swept through the street. Slowly all evidence of movement in this radiant advertisement to the world was gone. All that remained was the light looking at me with a sad glow. Before I could blink the illumination went dark. However, before it completely extinguished it whispered softly, "Go find the story. The end of an era has come, but a legacy is just beginning."

I looked closely at the small building in front of me. There was no one inside and it was evident to me now the barber pole had not been on. Could it have been my imagination playing with my senses? Only moments earlier I would swear I saw the bright light glowing behind those red, white, and blue stripes. The shop was clearly closed; no one was inside nor had they been. Yet, moments earlier I would have bet money it was.

Maybe while I was standing on the street, I became the victim of a day dream brought on by lack of sleep or the stress of the previous day's events. Perhaps, but something else clearly was going on. This tiny barber shop in this small town seemed to say, "Tell the world about the man whose name hangs on the storefront."

I stepped onto the sidewalk as my eyes made their way to the simple sign hanging in the window. I stared breathlessly as I read the words, "Gregory's Barber Shop."

It is an amazing journey this thing we call life. You never appreciate what is truly important to you until it seems too late. As the old saying goes, better late than never. I thought of this as I stood quietly on the lonely street realizing this vibrant hub of activity lay dormant.

How could a place with so many stories remain quiet? I needed to know, as Paul Harvey would have said, "The rest of the story." What drew me here on this day? I was determined to find the answer, but I was not prepared for the incredible truth I discovered along the way. To everyone else in the world, this was just a barber shop, but to me and the people in this small town, it was a place where inspiration met determination, where tragedy met comfort and where people came when they had nowhere else they could go.

This is the story of Americana at its finest. A beacon shining a light on a time we have forgotten, but would do well to remember and emulate. I was influenced by this place. I was touched by this man. I think after you read this story you will be as well. America, allow me to introduce you to Mr. Gregory, the barber.

My name is Jim and this is my story. I was born on August 2, 1941 in a small town in West Virginia. As a young boy, my favorite thing to do was go to my grandparents' house and hang out with my grandfather. He was such a big man with a heart of gold. I don't know if that was true for everyone, but it was for me. Of course, he thought I was the berries so maybe that influenced my decision somewhat. Nevertheless, he made a huge impact in my life when I was a young boy.

I grew up like most boys in a small town. I liked hunting, fishing, sports, and girls. I came from a patriotic household with great respect for the Armed Forces. I had one brother who joined the Army and another who was in the Navy. My father was also in the Army, so when I was old enough, I decided to follow in their footsteps and join the Army as well.

It was a given in my family you would spend some time serving your country. We felt we were so blessed to be free it was the least we could do. In fact one of my brothers fought in the Korean War. I always remember how proud I was of him because he served so courageously.

When I found out I was going to do my basic training at Fort Jackson in South Carolina I was actually quite enthusiastic about it. It was the same place my father went after he enlisted. I always wanted to follow in his footsteps, so I figured I was getting off to a good start.

After my training was complete, I was sent to Germany. The Berlin Crisis was in full swing, with the Soviets demanding the Western Allied forces leave West Berlin. They issued an ultimatum and we not only disregarded it, we brought in more troops to take control of the situation. The Cold War was in full bloom.

I spent eighteen months in Germany. For the most part, it was a good experience for me. I learned to work as part of a cohesive unit with my outfit and along the way I became educated in some areas about which I knew nothing before.

I don't know what it is about being a young soldier in a foreign land that makes you think you are invincible. I guess I just thought since I was an American with a shiny uniform I could do whatever I wanted and not have to face any consequences. Boy was I wrong.

On one evening, my buddies and I decided to go out for a night on the town at one of the local watering holes. I really hadn't drunk much of anything when I decided to get mouthy with one of the men in the bar. Sometimes youth and the uniform do not mix well and on this night it was most certainly the case.

The man had heard enough of my big mouth and decided he would put an end to it. You can imagine my surprise and fear when he pulled a .38 pistol from his coat and placed it directly into my chest.

"Have you ever seen the hole a bullet makes in someone when it goes right through them?" Those were the exact words that came out of his mouth, but he was not finished, he continued by saying, "Unless you shut your big fat mouth you are going to find out." Needless to say I got the message.

Most of my assignments during my time in Berlin centered on hauling ammunition. Thankfully, I never had to fight in a battle, but there was the one skirmish when someone ran into the back of me with their truck. I was sore but was not seriously injured. Not a pleasant experience to say the least.

Like I told you earlier, I always wanted to follow in my father's footsteps. He was in the Army, so I went into the Army. He trained at Fort Jackson and then I trained at Fort Jackson. When he got out of the military he became a barber, what did I do when I got out of the military, you guessed it. When I finished my service with the Army, I came back home and went to work in my dad's shop. I was going to be a barber.

My dad started the shop back in 1930. I joined the business in 1963. He cut hair for sixty-six years until he retired in 1996. On the door of the building, it stated we were open Tuesday through Saturday from 7 a.m. to 5 p.m., but I don't ever remember leaving at five o'clock and there were always people waiting to get in before seven in the morning.

One of the things you learn early on is the barber shop is not a politically correct environment. No topic was off limits and if you got offended, well, that was just too darn bad. This was a place where men were free to share their opinions without the PC police waiting at the door ready to give you a ticket. That is certainly a big problem with America today, too much political correctness going on.

When I started on my first day I can remember there were four chairs in the shop and three of us cutting hair; my dad, another guy named French and me. The first haircut I would ever deliver came early that morning. I still recall Mr. Mick, who was an older gentleman, walking into the shop, and sizing me up.

He said bluntly, "You going to cut hair boy?" I politely replied, "I am new." He just ignored my pleasantries and grumbled, "I just need a haircut not an explanation. Can you cut hair?" I said, "Yes sir." He smiled and said, "Well can you do it right now?" I was nervous and my words came out kind of choppy when I replied, "Yes sir I can do that for you. Please get in the chair."

From that day on I was the only person who cut Mr. Micks hair. Even on the day he died I was asked to come and cut his hair so it would look nice for the funeral. I really didn't mind. I figured it was the least I could do for a loyal customer who became a good friend.

It was not the only deceased person's hair I cut. I also made several trips to the homes of people who were too sick to come to the shop. In my day, doctor's made house calls, so why not a barber. It always seemed like the right thing to do.

I am not quite sure if what I experienced was unique to other barber shops in America, but they were certainly memorable events in my life. A week never went by without something out of the ordinary taking place.

Through the years, I always had folks who came to the shop to get a haircut who didn't have money to pay, but they always gave me something in return. It was not uncommon for guys to trade potatoes, beans, cucumbers, and tomatoes for a haircut. In fact, the shop was full of pictures or items from people who bartered for my services. I often had folks who couldn't afford to pay on this trip who paid me double the amount the next time in. There was a trust factor and I was glad for it. In fact, I accepted pretty much anything for a haircut, except on one specific occasion.

A gentleman, and I am using that term very loosely, entered the shop carrying a brown feed sack. He held the bag to his side with his arm extended so it did not touch his body. I told him, "Have a seat, you will be next." He didn't sit, he just stood there waiting. I just ignored him and went about cutting hair.

When I finished with the other customer I asked the man with the sack to sit down in the chair. He paused a moment and said, "I need to make a trade for a haircut, I don't have any money, but I do have this sack of rattlesnakes I can trade for one." He shook the bag and you could hear the rattle of the angered vipers. I looked at him and said, "Get yourself and that bag of reptiles out of here and don't come back until they are long gone." He calmly left the building and never came back. Not quite sure how other barbers would have handled that situation, but I wanted nothing to do with those snakes.

There were some folks who always got a free haircut from me. Even though this was not advertised, it was the rule in my shop. When a serviceman came in and sat down there was always an atmosphere of respect shown by everyone in the place. Men would ask where he did his training, where he was stationed, and how things were going for him.

Even though the names and locations were often different, the outcome was always the same. The serviceman got out of the chair after I removed the cloth and reached for his wallet. Sometimes before I could tell him it was no charge, another person would stand up and say, "Hey son, this haircut is on me. Thanks for your service to our country. We appreciate you." You could see the respect and gratitude light up the shop.

My dad instilled in me what it meant to be a patriot. It is not someone who stands behind the flag waving it all around, it is someone who stands in front of it willing to defend her at all costs. People all across this country who fight for the freedoms laid out by our Founding Fathers; they are patriots. I figured a free haircut was the least I could do for them.

I had some crazy days at the shop and met some crazy people. One day back in the early 1970s, I was standing behind the chair cutting hair when I noticed a lady weaving down the sidewalk. I could tell she was drunk, but I figured she knew where she was headed, so I went back about my business. A few seconds later I noticed she moved into the middle of the road where she proceeded to take off all of her clothes. She danced around for a moment or two and then left leaving her clothes behind. Needless to say the men were glued to the window.

She was not the only person to provide an interesting day for all in attendance. Ed and Fred were two local characters who were always getting themselves into sticky situations brought on by their own misdeeds. They worked for the local gas company and were genuinely good guys who found ways to get into mischief.

One weekday both of them came in for a haircut and it was not long before they shared a story with the folks at the shop. Ed started off on some tangent about all the beautiful women he knew and the two large bulls he owned. Fred grew tired of the nonsense, so he proceeded to get to the root of the topic as he shared the details of the event.

They were out doing their job for the gas company in their trac-tor trailer when the tail lights on the big rig quit working. They had no clue, until they were stopped by one of our fine men in blue. When he told them they had no tail lights they responded, "Yes we do." He said, "No you don't and you need to get it fixed right away." Ed said, "Well I can't get it fixed right way because you have us stopped. We have to go somewhere before we can have it fixed." The officer was not amused.

A day or two later after the incident they were stopped once again, but this time it was for speeding. The officer told Fred he was going fifty in a forty mph zone. Fred said, "Well, Ed told me the speed limit was fifty." The cop responded, "Well, your buddy lied to you it is only forty."

From here the story took a wild turn. Ed and Fred began to argue in front of the cop about what the actual speed limit on the sign said. So they agreed to ride with the officer back to the area where the sign was located and solve the argument there.

When they got back to the speed limit sign Ed pointed directly at it and said, "See it says fifty mph." The officer looked puzzled and said, "No that says forty mph, you are clearly wrong." Fred spoke up and said, "No he is right it does say fifty mph." They continued to argue with the officer until he finally decided to just give them a warning. I think they convinced him the sign did say the speed limit was fifty when in all actuality it really was forty.

They were a couple of good characters and they came in on a regular basis. They always had a story, but never caused me any trouble. Unfortunately, that was not the case with everyone. I have thrown out at least twenty drunks over the years who were disruptive to the operation of the shop. Most left quietly, but on at least three occasions I had to physically remove them. I guess all that good combat training from the Army came in handy after all.

Every day when I came home, I told my family about someone or something that occurred at the shop. It was our nightly dinner conversation. The stories were so many and even though some were negative I always tried to focus on a good one.

In a small town like ours you would never guess someone truly famous would come into your shop, let alone a four time Super Bowl winning quarterback. Imagine my surprise when Joe Montana and his son came in, sat down, and waited for a haircut. It turned out his son was going to West Virginia Wesleyan College for his senior year. It was an interesting and dynamic interaction to say the least. The funny thing about the whole experience was Joe explained specifically how I should cut his twenty-one year old son's hair. I chuckled to myself about the incident, because in my mind, a boy in college should be able to say how he wants his hair cut, but since his dad was paying I guess he got the last word.

It wasn't too busy a day, so I was able to get them taken care of in an efficient manner. Had they come in earlier on Saturday morning they would have had to wait for quite a while. We never played favorites at the shop. Everyone was equal and treated fairly.

Saturdays were usually our busiest day and people often said it took forever to finally get in the chair to get a haircut. On one occasion that was the case. An older gentleman who was a regular at the shop came in and sat down in his favorite chair. It was not long before he slumped over. A couple of guys at first thought he was sleeping until they nudged him and realized he was not asleep, he was dead. The paramedics came and tried to revive him, but it was to no avail.

Things like these are always going to be events you remember. In fact, everyone in the shop that day will remember it because Mr. Fallon passed away. There were other things I remember that were important to me others just looked past.

Even though Saturday was usually our busiest day and I never really got a chance to take a break, it was still my favorite day for one reason; my son came to the shop. Every Saturday my boy would ride his bicycle downtown to the little side street where the barber shop was located.

It was a big deal for him to come, but it meant so much more to me. He would arrive just before lunch time and I would always send him to get me something to eat. His favorite place to go was down to the local pool hall. They had the best hot dogs and my son thought it was neat to watch the guys shoot pool while my lunch was getting prepared. He always came back with a big smile on his face. He would place the hot dogs over by the counter so I could take a bite while I continued to cut hair. I never stopped to eat, I figured if there was someone in the chair waiting it was my job to take care of them.

As my son grew and started playing football in high school, Saturday became the day when he would come to the shop and everyone would go over every detail about Friday night's game. If anyone said my son made a mistake while playing I would always take up for him, but then later I would usually say, "You know he was right you did mess up and I think we need to talk about it." I just wanted my son to know I was his biggest fan and I had his back.

I always wanted my son to be a person who respected authority. I was determined to raise a responsible boy with a strong work ethic who looked out for his family. Sometimes the task came easy but on one particular occasion it was not a pleasant experience for either one of us.

It was a hot summer day when my son was somewhere around fifteen or sixteen years old, I don't remember his exact age. Nonetheless, I told him I needed him to trim the yard. He looked at me and said, "No, I am going to play basketball, I will do it later."

It wasn't so much the defiance of his response, but the attitude in which he delivered it. I looked him sternly in the eye and said, "No son you are going to do this now, then you can play basketball." He got right in my face and answered again, "No I am not, I told you I am going to play basketball."

This is not an easy thing to say, but I punched my son right in the mouth. I don't know if I did it because of his defiance or because I knew if he carried this attitude into his adult life he would probably end up as a thug or criminal. My son was shocked as he got off the ground with his lip bleeding. He slowly walked over to the shed and got out the weed eater. Later in the day I asked him if he was fine and he said, "I am good Dad, everything is OK."

It was the only time I ever stuck my son and it pained me to do it. Years later, when he was an adult he told me how that event affected his life for the positive. He shared how he gained respect for authority he was starting to challenge and how he learned to get his priorities straight; before you can play you must have your work done.

I am glad it worked out in the end because I had his best interest at heart even though what I did was probably not the best way to handle the situation, though my son says differently. He says it was exactly what he needed.

It was my goal to have a great relationship with him. I always wanted to spend time with my son from the time he was little to even now that he is a grown man. Over the years the activities have changed, but the desire to hang out with my boy has never diminished.

I can remember when he was in college. He came home one day and said he wanted to learn to scuba dive, so I said, "Okay, let's do it." He was shocked at first because he really just meant he was going to do it, but we ended up doing it together and it is a fond memory for us both.

One of the toughest things we probably ever did together was run a full marathon. It all began back years ago after I quit smoking. I smoked two packs of cigarettes a day for several years. It was just the thing to do back in my day. When I finally quit cold turkey, I began a fitness class at the college. I walked everyday around the indoor gym. Before long I was running around the place.

After a few years I worked my way up to a half marathon and then I decided I wanted to tackle a full marathon. If I was going to do this, there was only one marathon I wanted to run, the Marine Corps marathon in Washington, DC, and there was only one person I wanted there with me and that was my boy. He was a freshman in college at the time, but he willingly agreed to give it a go.

For one full year I got up every morning at 4:30 and ran with my son to prepare for the race. It was difficult, but the bonding experience we shared is one I will never forget. When the day finally came, I was so proud to run the race with him. How many kids would do this for their dad? It meant the world to me. We started at the National Cemetery and ended at the Iwo Jima Memorial. It was a patriot's dream.

As we neared the end of the race I decided to pick up the pace a little bit. My son, who is also competitive, began to speed up also. By the time we got to the end it was a dead out sprint, with me taking the lead. I know deep down my son backed off so I could finish first. He was just that kind of person.

For as long as I can remember he was always there with me no matter what transpired. Even as a small boy he would come to the shop on Monday and help me clean. I gave him a task of sweeping up the hair from behind the chairs and he always did a great job. It is a cherished memory even though to most it would mean nothing.

I always tried to take every opportunity that came along and use it as a learning experience for my boy. I took my responsibility as a dad very seriously and it seemed like something always happened at the barber shop that would lend itself to his education process.

When my son was a young lad he was in the shop one day when a couple of the guys were sitting around the checkerboard talking football. My son was a huge Dallas Cowboys fan, this was back in the day when Tom Landry was their coach. He was a great man of character.

After a short time my son began to say how the Cowboys were going to win the upcoming Sunday. Mr. Mick, one of the older fellas playing checkers told my son he was sorry, but that was not going to happen. Well, that got my son riled up and he began to argue with his elder to the point where a bet was placed. My son was willing to bet a quarter the Cowboys would win.

Since my son had no money he turned to me and asked if he could borrow a quarter. I said, "Here you go, now place your money on the table." He walked over and put it down. Mr. Mick pulled out a quarter and placed it on top of his and said, "OK, the bet is on. We will have your dad keep the money until after the game."

When the next week rolled around I knew my son would not look forward to coming to the shop because his beloved Dallas Cowboys lost the game. As he entered the door you could see the downcast look upon his face. Mr. Mick greeted him with the words, "So you lost the bet now didn't you." He walked over to me and I took out the quarters and said, "Okay son, take these over and give them to him." The old fella responded, "No, he doesn't have to pay me. We can just forget about it." I looked at Mr. Mick and replied, "No, he is going to pay you. He made the bet, he will pay."

My son made his way over to the gentleman and handed him the money. Mr. Mick gave him a big hug, rubbed his head and said, "Your father is trying to teach you right son. You listen to him." My boy smiled and looked at me before he headed for the door. Just about the time he grabbed the handle I said, "Hey, remember you still owe me a quarter. I loaned you the money to make the bet, but you have to pay me back your loan and I will be collecting interest." You could clearly see my son had lost all interest in gambling. He learned in an instant that if you are going to bet you better be prepared to lose because it will happen. It was a valuable lesson I wanted him to learn.

Another event that revolved around the barber shop was when he was old enough to drive. He borrowed my pickup truck to go fishing down at the lake with a buddy of his. He was pretty responsible most of the time so I did not worry, but he was a teenage boy, therefore I always had to be a little wary something might occur. On his way back from the lake he ended up putting the truck in the ditch along a back country road. After some time passed a well-tender came along. He offered to help pull them out. Evidently since my son had no money he told the guy if he came to town I would give him a free haircut if he mentioned he helped my son.

When my son came home that night and told me the entire story. He must have been a little nervous, because he washed the truck and had it shined before he told me what transpired earlier in the day. A few weeks passed when the man came into the shop and I gave him his free haircut. When I got home that night I said, "Hey, go get in your jar where you keep your money and get out enough for a haircut. Your buddy who pulled you out of the ditch came in to collect on your offer. Since you put the truck in the ditch, you can pay for it." My son, without hesitation, went to retrieve the money.

Later on, without him knowing, I put the money back in the jar. The money wasn't important to me, it was the lesson I wanted him to learn. If you make a mess out of something you have to accept the responsibility to pay for it. There are consequences for your actions.

★ ★ ★

Unfortunately, all of us experience heartache and tragedy throughout our lifetime. It is something we have to deal with, but it is never easy. Like I mentioned earlier I worked with my father who was a barber. I started at the shop in 1963 and worked with him until he passed away in 1990. It was a very hard day, because not only was he my dad, but he was my friend and partner in business. It was never quite the same after he was gone.

The shop was always a place of activity. Sure, guys came in to get a haircut, but many came in to just sit and talk. For quite some time we had a checkerboard set up in the shop for guys to play while waiting for a haircut.

Other guys came to have a place to go. They didn't want a haircut, they just wanted to be around people. I remember one guy who came early one Saturday morning and sat there all day up until closing time. When I got ready to lock up he asked if he could talk to me. I spent the next several hours playing counselor. That's not something they teach you in barber school, but it was a skill I cultivated over the years. I don't know how much I truly helped the guy, but he did leave there with a sense of help and peace. I was just glad to help a fellow person in need.

The shop became a place where people would come when they needed to be around their fellow man to seek comfort in a trying situation. That was never more evident than January of 2006. It was the day the Sago Mine exploded. The blast rocked our small community.

It was early Monday on January 2nd when word began to spread about the explosion at the Sago Mine. Thirteen miners were trapped inside and no one knew whether they were dead or alive. Reporters, news crews, and other interested folks poured into our community from all over the country.

When I opened the shop on Tuesday morning I had a line of guys waiting at the door to get in. However, not all of them wanted a haircut, many just wanted to talk about what was going on with the rescue operation. Guys came by to see what happened.

Before long, I had some of the national media guys sitting in my barber shop talking to the locals. They were getting firsthand information on each of the men who were trapped inside. It became the local hangout. I guess the town needed a place of tranquility after our community was turned upside down.

It was a tragic day when at first we learned all the miners had lived only to later learn twelve of the thirteen perished. People were angry, distraught, and confused. I remember well the absent look of the men in the shop who lost friends in the mine. It was a tough time, but somehow together we managed to get through. It seemed like every person in the town knew someone who was personally affected by the tragedy. I still remember it all like it was yesterday.

We all have hopes, dreams, and fears we experience in our lifetime. Unfortunately, one of my worst fears raised its ugly head in November 2013 when I received the words from my doctor, "Jim, I am sorry to tell you this, but you have cancer and the prospects are not good."

No one ever wants to hear such a diagnosis, but I have fought through many a challenge in my life, I figured I could fight one more. I knew the battle would be tough and there would be a chance I would lose, but I could not give up. At the very least I had to give it my all.

The radiation, the chemotherapy, and the lack of sleep really began to take its toll on me in no time. I was spending more time away from my beloved barber shop than I wanted. The days I was able to work I had people stopping in left and right just to visit. Some folks came by to get a haircut whether they needed it or not. I was not as quick as before, but I was still proficient and my customers left satisfied.

By the time June of 2014 arrived I was feeling pretty bad. The cancer was winning and I was spending way too much time at the hospital for my liking. I had lots of visitors. I loved having my wife and son sit by the bed and talk about anything. Their presence always made me smile.

One weekday afternoon while I was lying in the bed, my son and my nephew Greg came to visit me. They had not been there for very long when Greg asked, "Uncle, if there was ever somewhere you wanted to go or something you wanted to do what would that be?" I thought for a moment and said, "I don't know, I have lived a good life. Besides, I am not dead yet so let's not go there." He paused for a moment and replied, "I know that, but if there was any place in the world you would want to go, where would it be?"

I thought for a moment before I answered, but I knew deep down where I wanted to go. I looked at Greg and said, "I have always wanted to go to Pearl Harbor. I have always wanted to go and pay my respects to those guys who died for our freedom."

Since I was born in 1941 I considered the bombing of Pearl Harbor to be the watershed event in my lifetime. It was what defined my parent's generation, so in essence it also defined me.

When I finished talking, Greg looked me directly in the eye and said, "Okay, I will make it happen. I have plenty of frequent flyer miles, so I will send you and the whole family." My son at first was reluctant to take Greg up on his offer, but I insisted. I was not going to go if my boy was not going to be there. We always did everything together, so I was not about to let that change.

After they left the hospital I was not sure what would actually take place. I was not even sure Greg was serious, but deep down I believed he was. What I did not know was just how serious they were. Greg's wife began working all her social media contacts, letting people know about the fundraising site they created so folks could donate. All of this was done without my knowledge, but I knew they were up to something.

By the time the end of June rolled around I was feeling really bad. In fact, I could hardly even walk, let alone stand for any amount of time. I remember the last haircut I gave at the barber shop. Rod Kimble came in that day and waited until the very end. It took me a while but he did not seem to mind. When I was finished, we both walked out and he locked the door for me. It would be the last time I cut hair in my shop. For me, the twisting, turning whirl of the barber pole came to an end.

It was a very sad event for me, but a few days later, one of the greatest moments of my life took place. On July 2nd a limo arrived at my home. I was informed by my wife we were headed to a party. Who doesn't love a party? Needless to say, I was all in for the fun.

The trip was a short one, only about two miles, but what I saw at the destination brought me to tears. Just outside my small town barber shop was a huge street party. The citizens of the community put together an event to honor me. Words can't express the emotion that came over me.

John Jenkins who owns the local Ford Dealership had the Wounded Warrior Ford Mustang brought to town. I got to personally sign my name on the car. It was quite an honor. Downtown, there was a live band playing. Businesses from all over the community donated food and refreshments. Never a man felt more loved than I did.

My two beautiful granddaughters came inside the shop with me. I can't even describe the way I felt as they stood by me while I sat in my barber chair. How could a man be so blessed?

I have always been a lover of motorcycles, so you can understand my elation when they brought that incredible custom Boston Red Sox chopper over to me. I knew I would be unable to ride it, but just sitting next to that thing of beauty was such a thrill.

My son touched me on the shoulder and said, "What do you think Pop?" I could not answer, I was too choked up, but had words come out, I would have said, "Son, you are one of the true blessings God has provided to me in this life. I love you boy!"

The party was amazing, but little did I know it was only the beginning. Imagine my surprise when my son told me, "Dad, we are scheduled to catch a flight to Hawaii this Saturday. We are heading to Pearl Harbor." Of course, I was overcome with emotion. I was just a barber, how could this group of people care so much for me?

The flight was not an easy one. I tried to hold my own, but deep down I knew I was not well. As soon as we arrived on the island I was treated like a king. They greeted me with fan fair like I was a visiting dignitary. I appreciated the reception greatly, but I knew where I wanted to go. I had to see Pearl Harbor.

On the 5th of July we headed to the Arizona Memorial. I can remember watching the story about the bombing of Pearl Harbor. It was quite emotional for me, but nothing compared to rolling my wheelchair out onto the platform of the memorial. The sky was a beautiful azure blue without a cloud anywhere to be seen. I knew this event would be a milestone in my life.

I positioned my chair as close to the rail as possible, then locked the wheels into position. I took both hands and placed them firmly on the railing in front of me. I could not come all this way and not stand to honor these brave men. With every ounce of strength I had,

I pulled myself up into a standing position and looked over the edge down into the depths of that sunken ship.

The wind blew slightly over my shoulder as I removed my hat placing it over my heart. As a lone tear raced down my cheek I humbly said to the men who were buried below, "Thank you, what a brave bunch of men you must have been. Don't worry guys, our flag is still there."

After a brief prayer and my very best salute I said goodbye and lowered myself down into my wheelchair. I was done. My life had come full circle. Later that night I sat on the balcony of my hotel room overlooking the ocean with my son. I knew at that moment it would not be long. My son didn't want to hear me talk that way, but we both knew the truth; I was dying and my time was growing short.

We came back from Hawaii on July the 16th. It is now July 24th and I know I am not long for this world but I am so grateful for all the wonderful people I have known throughout the years who have been so good to me and my family. For that I am extremely grateful.

The last person's hair I would ever cut was my son Jim's and it was at my house on the back porch. I just wanted one last opportunity to do something meaningful with him. I love that boy more than he could ever know.

To everyone who cared for me and my family I leave you one simple truth. Don't ever forget who you are and what you are.

As I sat with Jim during the last few days of his life here on earth I asked him a simple question, "Are you glad you were a barber?" He looked at me with eyes full of tears and proudly stated, "I am so glad I was a barber."

After those words I slowly closed my laptop and thought to myself, "Yes Jim, I too am glad you were a barber. To some, you may have just cut hair, but to me and the people of this town you were so much more."

★ ★ ★

Sadly, on August 6th Jim Gregory Sr. passed away, but he has left behind a legacy few could have ever imagined.

I remember quite fondly as a young man sitting in the barber shop watching Jim cut hair when a car pulled up on the street outside the shop. Jim quietly excused himself and went out to open the door of the vehicle. He proceeded to assist an elderly gentleman into the shop and then returned to tell the person in the driver's seat what time they should come back.

I was struck by the care and concern a simple barber would show for a customer who was going to give him a few bucks for a haircut. It cost only three dollars at that point in time, but that did not matter. Jim cared for the man and it clearly showed.

He didn't just cut hair to make a living, he cut hair because he loved people. He genuinely enjoyed getting to know them. Look all over this town and you will see people whose lives were impacted by this local barber.

The little building with the red, white, and blue pole on the side was more than a barber shop, in essence it was a schoolhouse. Many a lesson was taught, but no homework was ever given. Respect, honor, and character ruled the classroom of this learning center.

Gregory's Barber Shop defined a time I am afraid we have forgotten. In the day and age of Facebook, Twitter, and Instagram, the world has traded genuine human contact for a counterfeit electronic one. The real social network is the one where we are actively involved in the lives of others. Simply put, loving our neighbor as we love ourselves.

Thank you Jim for the impact you made on one small boy who sat in your barber chair. I will be forever grateful for your service to our community. I will see you on the other side.

Oh Say Does That

Drops of sweat dripped down my face as I looked at the woman lying on the ground. I fell to my knees and searched for a pulse on her wrist. As my fingers gripped, I begged God to let me feel even the faintest heartbeat, unfortunately I felt nothing. Immediately, I placed my hands on her chest and began to press and release in a systematic rhythm. With every movement I knew I was battling the clock. I counted, one, two, three, then grabbed the back of her head and blew air into her mouth. A woman's life hung in the balance and the future of her family rested in my ability, an eighteen year old kid. My name is Peter and this is my story.

They say ordinary people can do extraordinary things. I don't know if that is true or not, but I do know I was born as an ordinary baby boy on September 1st in Bronxville, New York. My father was a letter carrier and his career kept us in this general vicinity most of my childhood years.

It is quite amazing to me how little things you do lead you down the path of life's journey. Each step along the way is like a string of dominos. One knocks over the other until you get to the end. It moves along so fast that if you blink you will miss something important along the way.

As a young boy, we lived near the Kensico Dam just outside Valhalla, New York. It was a massive granite structure built in 1915.

I remember my friends and me climbing up the side of those rock walls. Since the dam curved at the top we could never reach the precipice, but it was an enjoyable feat for young boys trying to become men. Each stone crevice provided a place for a hand to grasp. Maybe we were foolish, the damn was over 100 yards high but the thought of getting hurt rarely ever crossed our minds. Why climb the dam you might ask? The answer for me was easy; it was there, why not!

The thrill of scaling the walls of this water retaining fortress led me to take the next logical step in my life's progression of dominos. I joined the Civil Air Patrol. At the ripe old age of fourteen, I was introduced to the world of search and rescue, as well as other quasi-military activities. I loved every minute of it. By the time I was sixteen, I was the Cadet Commander on an International Air Cadet Exchange with Canada.

The things I learned were incredible. Search and rescue was an electrifying atmosphere for me throughout my teenage years. Looking back now, most of the events seem quite small but at the time they were larger than life. However, there was one experience I will never forget.

We received a call about a small plane that went down just outside the Westchester County Airport. Within minutes our entire search and rescue team was loaded and ready to spring into action. The senior members of the Civil Air Patrol took to the air. Their mission was to fly over the area of the crash site and look for any debris which could lead us to those on board the aircraft. I was a member of the ground team. It was our job to comb the area looking for any signs of survivors.

The forest felt very dense as we made our way through the cluster of seventy foot pines. From the information we received from the team in the air we knew we should start to see objects come into view before we went much further. Our group did a sector grid search, which meant each team had a specific sector in which they traversed looking for any sign of human life. It did not take us very long until we found our first piece of the aircraft. It was a small section of the tail, but it told us we were heading in the right direction.

With every passing footstep my mind began to wonder, *What would we find at the end of this journey*. All I could do was pray for the best.

Over the course of the next several hundred yards we found more pieces of debris. From these pieces of the puzzle it was easy to see what happened. Heading toward the Westchester County Airport, the plane traveled over the Kensico Reservoir, flew past the dam and then began its approach for the runway. However, the pilot misjudged the landing, so they hit a massive expanse of pines. The force of the plane striking the sixty to seventy foot trees caused it to break apart into small sections.

The scraps of twisted metal led us along a trail of destruction until we reached the fuselage of the Cessna 172. It was a single engine, high winged plane that could hold four passengers. As I raced toward the downed unit, my heart began to race. I was unsure of what I would see inside.

When I got to the door I looked inside the cockpit and found two men strapped in their seats. They were both dead. Well, that is what I thought at first. Instinctively I tapped one of them on the shoulder a couple of times and miraculously he responded. He was alive. My cousin, who was also a part of the search and rescue team, did the same thing to the other man in the cockpit. He did not respond at first, but within a few minutes he opened his eyes. Both men were pretty banged up, but they survived.

It was quite a rarity for people to walk away from such an accident. Since the cabin of the plane stayed intact, it provided a protective shelter for them as they descended through the dense forest. I don't know how it happened, but I thanked God it did. Had the cockpit broke apart, we would have probably only found pieces of the passengers.

This was not the only adventure I would face during those formative years of life. It was about five weeks after this plane crash when another character building experience took place as I was coming back from drill and ceremony training. While traveling down one of the New York parkways heading toward the city, the car in front of me lost control and went off the road. Time seemed to move in slow motion as I watched the vehicle hit an embankment and flip into the air. With a tremendous thud the car came to rest upside down.

The palms of my hands began to sweat as they gripped the steering wheel tightly. Immediately, I pulled over to the side of the road and stopped my vehicle. With no thought for our own safety, my younger brother and I jumped out of the car. The other two cadets with us where terrified and paralyzed with fear because of what they just witnessed. I knew they would be of no help in such a situation so I told them to remain inside.

My brother began to direct traffic as I made my way toward the accident. My adrenaline was racing at break neck speed as my life saving instincts took over. The asphalt under my feet felt like quicksand as I raced over to the mangled, upside down automobile. I knew what I might find inside could be horrific, but it did not matter.

When I finally reached the car, I realized the engine was revving at full speed. I reached my hand through the shards of broken glass of what was once a side window. As I slid my fingers past the steering column I felt the keys still in the ignition. With a quick twist and pull I removed them, but it made no difference, the motor was still engaged and running at full revs.

The sound was almost deafening, but what I smelled told me I had bigger issues. Gasoline was leaking from the carburetor. A puddle formed under the car and I was standing in it. I knew if the car caught fire, not only would the passengers perish, but so would I.

When I looked inside the car I could see the passengers hanging upside down still strapped into their seats. They were an elderly couple, probably in their early eighties. I did my best to free the passenger first because she was in worse condition, but because of the pressure of her body, I could not unbuckle the seat belt. The insanity of the situation was overwhelming. With every passing second the sound of the engine and the smell of the leaking fuel told me time was not on my side.

Instinctively, I reached inside my pocket and took out my knife. The fabric of the seatbelt was formidable, but I managed to cut through it. Now that I had the passenger free, I dragged her over to safety and raced back for the driver. I found the same situation as the first, the seat belt would not disengage so I would have to cut him out.

The engine was getting hotter, you could literally feel the heat coming through the broken windshield. I was losing the race, but I knew I could not give up. Both our lives depended on me cutting through the seatbelt. I was not about to leave him to die. If the car caught fire, we were going to die together. Abandoning him was not an option.

Finally, after much persistence, the seat belt was severed. I wrapped my arms around the elderly man and carried him from the car. We were a few feet away when the inevitable happened; the car ignited from the gasoline and caught fire. Immediately, the entire vehicle was engulfed in flames. As I looked back I realized where I stood only moments earlier was now a searing, burning inferno. By the grace of God, both of our lives were spared.

Most people never experience a situation like that in their entire lifetime, yet I was constantly finding myself in situations where I would play the role of rescuer. My life was becoming a real life version of the 1970s TV show, *Emergency*. Little did I know this was only the beginning!

Since rescuing people was in my blood, it only made sense to make my services available to the Volunteer Ambulance Corps. This proved to be both rewarding and life changing. I was still a teenager when I first joined the unit. The training I received proved irreplaceable. To me, there was nothing better than knowing I could help save a person who was in a life threatening situation.

For a volunteer group, our response time was incredible. For the majority of our calls we were able to respond within about three minutes. Time is so critical, especially when dealing with a heart attack situation.

I remember in the summer of 1982, a call came in from only about a quarter of a mile from my house. Since I was so close, I went straight to the residence and the ambulance met me at the location.

When I arrived at the address, Gary, a friend of mine from high school came through the doorway in a panic. When he saw me, he was quite confused and he asked, "Peter, what are you doing here?" I told him, "I am with the Ambulance Corps, a call came in that some- one had a heart attack."

Gary was frightened and panicked. His face exhibited a pale, desperate look of despair. He began to cry as he led me to his mother. When we got to the kitchen I found Gary's mom face down on the floor, not moving. The situation was not a good one.

I rolled her over and immediately checked her pulse. She had none. I listened carefully to see if she was breathing; not a breath. I quickly and instinctively began to administer CPR to his mom. I counted as I systematically pushed on her chest. This was not just anyone, this was Gary's mom. I knew I must do my best to save her.

I could hear the sound of the sirens as the other two guys on the Ambulance Corps arrived. They rushed into the room to find me working on the lady. I continued pressing on her chest as I told them the situation. Then it happened, the greatest thing occurred. Her heart began to beat as she began to breathe. Gary's mom was alive. She began to cough and sputter as her body began to restart her vital engines of life. The crew then took over. They got her stable and prepped for a trip to the hospital.

I cannot not even tell you how good I felt, nor how happy my friend Gary was that I was there. He was the youngest of fourteen children and we still keep in touch to this day. His mom has since passed away. She was ninety-two when she died; she lived thirty years after her heart attack. Nothing will ever take away the look I saw on Gary's face when his mother regained her life. It was a priceless experience and I thank God I was there.

I had the good fortune of rescuing at least twelve people who were heart attack victims. Those were joyous moments indeed, but a darker day was just around the corner. It all began a few days before September 1st, 1983, when my mother came to me and said, "Peter, you are going to get shot. I saw it right before my eyes as if it was a vision of the future. I want to warn you that you are going to get shot."

Now there is nothing like being told a piece of news like that to set your mind going the wrong direction. I looked at her and said, "Gee thanks mom, I really appreciate that. I have just graduated high school, I plan on starting college this fall and now you tell me I am going to die." She paused and stated, "I did not say you were going to die, I only said you are going to get shot sometime. I don't know when and I don't know how or why, but I truly feel like it will happen."

Needless to say I felt really insecure, so I decided I needed to pay a visit to a man of God. As we sat down and began our conversation I had several questions about where my life was going. I told him all about what my mother told me. I was upset about what that event would do to them if I died. I had so many questions and no real answers.

He gave me some really good words of wisdom. He said, "Peter, you have to focus on what God wants you to do and not worry about everyone else because you are going to screw it up. It does not matter what happens in this life to you. You are here for a purpose and it is God's purpose. Do not worry about the consequences along the way because God is going to be there looking out for you." I listened carefully to those words and realized how valuable they would be to me just two days later on September 1st.

On that fateful day I celebrated my nineteenth birthday, unfortunately it was far from a time of celebration. It turned into a day of tragedy.

It all began with the first call we received. A gentleman contacted the West Chester County medical center telling them he thought he was having a stroke. Immediately the medical personnel who answered the phone took the man's information. As the lady began to talk to the man she realized he was just a few blocks away, so she encouraged him to walk to the facility. She figured he could get there sooner than the Ambulance Corps could arrive at his home.

This was a very bad decision, because once we finally received the call and arrived on the scene at the medical center we found the guy outside, laying on the ground. The medical attendant he called was standing over him. Not only had the man had a stroke, he also had a heart attack.

Without a moment to spare I sprang into action and began the lifesaving procedures I performed successfully on twelve other occasions. Unfortunately, there was no hope, the man was already gone. There was nothing I could do to rescue him. The man was dead.

I said nothing on our way back to the unit. It was a very somber moment for me. I had never lost a patient. It did not matter it was not my fault, it did not matter the medical attendant never should have had the guy try to walk to the facility. In my mind I failed. In fact, all of us felt depressed. My cousin Dave, my friend Rich, and I were all friends from high school. We had just experienced an event that would affect us for the rest of our lives.

After arriving back at our base of operations, we were there for no more than twenty-five minutes when another call came in. We quickly hit the road and headed to the location. When we arrived at the Independent Living Facility, we rushed straight inside. The gentleman we were there to assist was about seventy years old. His wife told us she was sure he had a heart attack.

As we approached the man we could see he was unresponsive and lying on the floor. I began CPR procedures immediately. Nothing was happening. With no other course of action available we decided to transport this man to the hospital so we loaded him into the back of the unit and sped off.

The ambulance raced along with lights flashing and sirens blaring. I was in the back working on the gentleman. One, two, three, and then a breath. Nothing. Not one single sign of life. I kept trying. I was doing everything I was trained to do. Why was I not saving this guy? Why was he not regaining consciousness? When we arrived at the hospital, we rushed him inside. It was all to no avail, the man did not make it.

The ride back to our facility was depressing. We were up to bat twice on the day and both times we struck out. I was feeling especially down because I performed CPR applications on two calls and the result was two deaths.

When we arrived back at our home location the entire place seemed dark and dreary to me. The mood was somber and bleak. I could not snap out of my depression. Unfortunately, things would go from bad to worse when the next call come in.

When the address was read, I froze. I re-read the number of the house, I reassessed the city. This was not just any location; this was the home of my grandfather. The details were sketchy, but we did know for certain someone at that location had just suffered a heart attack.

My mind raced with desperation and despair as we dashed to the home of my grandfather. I was so stressed, but my cousin Dave told me, "Peter, relax. It does not matter who is out there, we have done this many times. Everything will be okay." His words brought some comfort, but I was certainly feeling uneasy about the entire situation.

When we arrived, I saw my grandfather standing in the door looking lost, dazed, and confused. Since it was not him in trouble, I realized that it was probably my step grandmother. They had not been married for very long, but the lady still held a special place in my heart. Needless to say she was very important to my grandfather. In fact, I was scheduled to have dinner with them the following evening.

When we got inside I found her lying face down in the bathtub. The police were already on the scene. When they realized she wasn't breathing they strapped an oxygen mask on her, but they did nothing else. In fact, when I walked in they were standing around telling jokes.

I was livid, I said, "What in the world do you think you are doing?" One of the officers got mouthy with me and stated, "Cool it kid, we gave the old lady some air." Those were not the right words to say to me in this situation. I responded in a less than professional manner as my fist struck the officer in the face. Blood flew everywhere as he hit the ground. I knew it was not the right thing to do, but I let my emotions get the better of me. Fortunately for me, my grandfather was best friends with the Chief of Police so nothing ever came of the incident.

Let me clearly state I have great respect for the men who wear the badge. Some of my best friends are police officers, but on this occasion the insensitivity shown by this person really hit me the wrong way. I realize now I responded poorly to the situation at hand.

After the punch was thrown people scrambled between us as I reached over to get my step grandmother out of the tub and onto the floor. I began CPR procedures at once. I was not about to let her die. My crew brought in the cart and loaded her up as I continued.

Once again, off we raced to the medical center. I was desperate; one, two, three then breathe. I had to succeed, I could not fail. My grandfather needed her and I could not let him or her down. I had to save her life. I did everything I knew how to do, but it did not matter, she was dead by the time we arrived at the hospital. I was zero for three on the day.

I took all of those deaths very personal. I had never had anyone die on any of my calls and everyone I touched or September 1st, 1983 ended up deceased. It really affected me hard.

At my shift's end I decided I needed some more words of wisdom, so I headed back to speak to the spiritual leader of my church. When I walked in, he could tell I was distraught. After telling him about my day I said, "This is all my fault. I have all this training and I can do all these things. I should be able to save them."

As soon as I finished speaking those words, he stopped me and boldly stated, "Do you really think you can save anybody? Did you die on a cross for anyone's sins?" I immediately spoke up and said, "No that is not what I meant." He cut me off mid-sentence with the words, "I know what you meant and you are wrong. Saving is not your department. You can be an instrument of God to rescue, but in the end it is up to Him to save."

We continued to talk for quite some time and before long I realized my life does have a purpose. I might not ever know what it is, but God has allowed me to be placed in situations resulting in the greater good. I may never be able to fathom what God is doing or even begin to figure it out. My job is simply to listen, follow through and trust.

After the conversation and much prayer, I decided my life needed a new turn. I had had enough of death in my life so I made up my mind on that day I would join the Army. There's nothing like getting out of the frying pan and jumping right into the fire.

Life in the military for me began at Fort Benning, Georgia or the Benning School for Boys as we called it. I went through sixteen weeks of straight infantry training, then it was off to airborne school. Since I spent time in the Civil Air Patrol as a teenager, being in the air would not be a big deal.

Once I finished airborne school, I headed for my first tour of duty in Hawaii. It would prove to be a rough assignment. Funny huh? The time I spent on the island was actually quite enjoyable, but when we left there, things often turned quite dicey.

From the Hawaiian base of operations I spent time in the Philippines, Thailand, Australia, Japan, Korea, Guam, Wake Island, and Alaska, just to name a few. My first major deployment was when we headed to Mindanao in the Philippines where we fought with some special forces from the seventh group. Our job was to assist in fighting the Islamic extremists who were terrorizing the local villages. We were there to kill the bad guys, but there was only one hitch, no one was allowed to know we were there. Our assignment was a secret one. At the time, the government feared we would kick off an international incident if the world knew about our mission.

Not all of my duties were quite so secretive or glamorous as some might say. I can remember specifically having to guard ammunition and weapons at Subic Bay in the Philippines, which is just north of Manila. That mission proved to be an interesting one.

One night while on assignment, I became aware of someone on the dock who was acting quite suspiciously. As I made my way toward the suspect I soon realized he was trying to blow up the ammunition depot. When he spotted me coming his way he quickly bolted from the scene. Immediately, the chase was on. It did not take long for me to flush him out into the open. The shore patrol came by and quickly picked him up. I am not sure whatever happened to him or better stated, it is probably best if I don't tell you what happened to him.

Every day was certainly different. Some were full of drama and others bordered on the lighter side. On one afternoon, a soldier was down near the jungle making faces and taunting the monkeys. Now this was strictly forbidden. In fact during one of our safety briefings they specifically told us not to mess with the monkeys.

Evidently, this soldier ignored the warning or he felt he knew better. We tried several times to warn him saying, "Hey dude, don't mess with the monkeys." We soon realized our words fell on deaf ears as he yelled, "Aww shut up!" As he turned back to throw rocks, a massive hail storm of rocks came flying out of the jungle directly at him. Stones reigned down all around the soldier. The monkeys were pelting him with rocks left and right.

The other guard on duty and I began to laugh. I thought how funny this situation was. I bellowed out loud, "That is what you get, throw one rock and get five hundred in return. I told you, don't mess with the monkeys."

Once again, my warning landed upon deaf ears as the guy walked over to the edge of the jungle and proceeded to scream in the direction of the monkeys. This was a very bad idea. Within seconds a huge rustle began in the trees. The next thing I knew, the man began to scream as he turned to run. It seemed like every monkey in the jungle had come forth to chase him.

At first, we began to laugh until we soon realized he was heading our way and so were about a thousand angry monkeys. I had no clue what to do. Rapidly, I began to move in the opposite direction until I reached the end of the pier where I proceeded to jump into the water.

The maneuver proved to be effective. I can still see the hilarious picture in my mind. I was standing in the bay with my rifle held above my head with a thousand screaming monkeys on the dock. There I would remain until they finally decided to head back into the jungle. So the moral of this story is a simple one. Don't EVER throw rocks at the monkeys.

I spent a total of four years in Hawaii and from there I went to Colorado Springs before moving on to the Recruiting Command Division in Wisconsin. I had the largest area by land mass in the nation for recruitment. However, I had the smallest towns as well. Some of the high schools only had five or six kids in their graduating class. Towns like Peterson, Minnesota which had a population of two hundred ninety-five at the time with just seventeen kids in the entire high school. Needless to say, I did not have a lot of prospects.

The number one thing I learned throughout this whole process was never to lie to a kid about the Army. I saw far too many recruiters do that. I wanted no part of it. I had ethics and unfortunately many recruiters did not. It was all just a numbers game to them. I figured if I told a kid the truth about what to expect, they would be better prepared for what was coming. I told them both the good and the bad. I did not sugar coat anything.

After it was determined recruitment and me were not a good match, I headed back to Fort Carson in Colorado before leaving the Army entirely. I was not out for very long until I decided maybe a stint in the Army Reserve would be a good plan.

I was originally with a unit in Connecticut before I got transferred over to New York. I was a member of the 77th division which was known as the Statue of Liberty division. Life in the Reserves was quite good. In fact I found I liked it just as much as I did the Army. For the most part everything was routine and nothing much happened, but that all changed in September 2001. My world and everyone else's was about to be rocked.

☆ ☆ ☆

I got up early that morning. I had plans for the evening so I knew I needed to get an early start to my day. When I arrived at the office I began coordinating everything we needed to accomplish.

I was the sergeant in charge of the Operations Division. Readiness and Intelligence NCO was my official government title. The day was totally normal until we got the word a plane ran into the World Trade Center in New York City. Immediately, we thought the information must be wrong, because it was a clear day.

We then began to discuss the time when a plane accidently ran into the Empire State building. We knew that was a clear day as well, so we decided it was plausible for this to be an accident. However, after some thought, we began to think otherwise. The Empire State Building was made completely out of granite where the World Trade

Centers were basically hollow shells with walls hung on the outside. This began to raise a red flag to us.

We had recently placed a television in the operations building, so we watched the live coverage. When we saw the footage, we knew this did not look right. Immediately, we called our commanders and sounded the alarm that we thought something was going down. This was no accident.

Our suspicions were confirmed when the second plane hit the other Trade Center tower about fifteen minutes later. We had been attacked. Without a moment to spare, our base was locked down for security purposes.

Since my unit was part of defense intelligence we were aware of the possibility for such an intrusion. For weeks we had been getting information about a possible attack, but no specifics were uncovered. It was the responsibility of the FBI to share this information with the appropriate organizations. Whether they did or didn't I don't know, but it was clear on that day several of those organizations were not prepared to deal with the threat.

The information shared with the public at large and what is truth is not always the same thing. In fact, the official Army line states no federal forces were at Ground Zero on September 11, 2001. However, I know that is not the case, because I and a small group headed down there in our trucks. The only vehicles that could really move around were military, police or emergency service units. Everything else was simply a parking lot for about thirty miles outside the city. Nothing was moving.

We drove on the shoulders of the road, on sidewalks, and anywhere else we wanted. We had a mission to serve and we were not about to be deterred. When we arrived just outside World Trade Center 7, where the CIA is held, we stopped, and exited the vehicle. We were there for no more than ten minutes when the terrible happened; the building collapsed right before us.

The force of the building coming down was felt throughout my entire body. If that was not bad enough, the smell was even worse. It was a combination of rotten eggs and decaying corpses mixed with burning plastic. It was absolutely horrible. To this day I cannot get the stench out of my mind.

There was no running or time to take cover when the building fell. We were immediately covered from head to toe with the dust, soot, and debris of World Trade Center 7.

Instinctively we raced to the pile and began to dig trying desperately to find anyone alive. It was such a futile effort. Twisted metal, stone, and wire were wrapped around one another in a conglomeration of destruction. It was horrible to remove what you thought was a piece of the building and you realized you were holding the detached limb of someone buried beneath the rubble.

Things moved slowly until the Teamsters arrived with their heavy equipment. Many of the guys were devastated by what they saw, because many of them built those buildings. It was a very emotional time for everyone involved.

As we dug through the remnant of the building, we soon discovered there were fires burning beneath. I have no explanation for why that was the case, but the whole incident was incredibly strange. There should have been no fires unless there was something inside that was used for an incendiary device. When a building falls it is just mounds of debris, but this one fell and it burned for days. I have no answer for that, it is just what I experienced. The whole day was full of questions with very few answers.

We dug throughout the entire evening and into the night. We stopped periodically for rest and when we did the entire place was eerily silent. You could sense the fires and hear your heartbeat. The purpose of our stoppage was to determine if we could hear any survivors. It was a chilling event to wait and listen hoping to hear someone calling for help. It was a horrible feeling.

Unfortunately, on my side of the building we found no one alive. At one point I stepped on a forearm and hand with a wedding band on it. It was a sickening sensation. The entire arm was charred all the way through. This was someone's spouse and they died needlessly at the hands of the vilest group of cowards Hell ever produced.

The people I found in the pile I did not know, but there were thirty-four reserve soldiers who were part of the Port Authority PD, NYPD, and the FDNY I knew very well. They were all consumed by the buildings when they collapsed. I cannot express the grief I felt then and still do to this day. For the next six to eight weeks I went to a lot of funerals. It was gut-wrenching to say the least. Every funeral had bagpipe players and to this day I have yet to play the bagpipes again.

For the next two years I helped manage a lot of the recovery operations going on at Ground Zero. Every day it seemed like another terrible story arose from the debris. It was a day I was sure we would never forget, but viewing recent events, I am afraid we have. The enemy is real and appeasement will gain us all an early grave.

Once my tour of duty was finished in New York, I was transferred down to Fort Belvoir, Virginia for about a year. I got orders to go to the Joint Task Force for Global Network Operations. During my time in New York, I was doing both Operations and Intelligence so the Army thought this was a perfect fit.

The first day I walked in, there was a gentleman who was with me at the same operation in New York. He walked right over and said, "Hi Peter, I am glad you got here. I asked for you specifically. You are the right person for this job." I was kind of floored, because I did not know exactly what the job even entailed.

I soon learned I would be working with applied technologies in the field of active computer defense. In a nutshell, Cyber Security. This was clearly to my liking. Before long, I developed some pretty sophisticated algorithms for network defense. Weeks later, at a briefing, several senior members of the Defense Department began to ask me detailed questions about my project. You could clearly tell they were interested.

About two weeks later, I found out just how truly fascinated they were about what I shared. I received a nice letter stating that for the good of the Army I was being reassigned to the Intelligence Branch. Weeks later, I was in training, and upon graduation I was told to report to the National Security Agency or NSA for short.

My initial response was not a good one. It was a sixty-five mile drive one way from my home to NSA. I pleaded my case, gave several good reasons why I should stay at Fort Belvoir and I ended up at NSA. The Army ruled the chess board and I was merely a pawn in the grand scheme of the game.

This was certainly a whole new ball game for me. I ended up working in several different departments while there. Computer Network Operations, Electronic Warfare, Operations Security, Military Deception, and Psychological Operations, to name a few. As you can imagine I can share absolutely NOTHING with you about what I did for NSA.

I can say I got a lot of schooling in deception and I had the opportunity to apply many of those concepts and theories in my everyday work life. I am sure you have heard the saying, "Perception is reality," well I was living in a world where deception was reality. The words used to gather information could seem like a simple phrase, but a deeper meaning was usually known to the one executing the deception.

Unfortunately, this game was often played within the organization as well. It made it very difficult to maintain an ethical sense of values when you were constantly deceiving those around you. Most of the folks I worked with were very good people who wanted to do what was best for our country, but there were some who had other agendas. Their selfish motives often won the day and that left me feeling very empty.

Eventually I had to walk away from the agency. I could not live in a situation where everyone says, "I trust you," while lying to you in the same sentence. Everyone walked around smiling like it was all good.

Throughout my time at NSA, I became disgusted at the things perpetrated by the government on innocent people. All my fears about a government transforming from a benevolent partner to a malevolent dictator were happening right before my very eyes. I could see where we were going and how fast we were getting there and I knew deep down I could not be a part.

It was not long thereafter that I began working as a Senior Combat Developer for the Army Cyber Command. My job was to create different kinds of cyber-attack or defense tools for the military. I did that until I took over the Counter Intelligence Office at the Army Research Laboratory.

This proved to be really interesting. In fact we were very successful in nabbing a few bad guys who here hell-bent on causing physical harm to American citizens. We set up a cyber counter intelligence system. The system was not deployed very long before we caught some guys spying for countries that did not have our best interest at heart. In a very short time we managed to catch four individuals. The project proved to be very successful. In fact, at the time, we did better than any other cyber intelligence office in the entire United States.

I have always been an individual who not only wanted to help my country, but I loved being in situations where I could help others who were in trouble. In fact, I worked for a short period of time with INTERPOL, which is the International Criminal Police Organization. I handled human trafficking and the prevention thereof. This proved to be a very difficult and depressing position.

You literally can't save eighty percent of the people. In fact, it makes you sick to your stomach. There were times I could not eat for a week because I was so disgusted at what I experienced. It affects everything you do and you constantly think about it day and night. You constantly questioned yourself, "Had I done this different, then maybe I could have saved them." It was a miserable existence.

The only way I managed to get through each day was to remember the words I heard years earlier in church when I was nineteen. "Peter, you cannot save people only God can, but you are here for a purpose. You might not know what it is, but you are part of a larger plan." I hung on those words every time a mission did not go as outlined. I might have felt like a failure but I knew deep down that even though I did not understand everything I could trust in the One who holds the whole world in His hands.

Sometimes you win the battle and sometimes you lose, but I do remember one day our mission was both a success and a failure at the same time.

Through some creative information gathering we found out about a shipment of young women who were coming into a United States port via a shipping container. The ages of the girls were anywhere from young teens to the mid-twenties. They were sold in Asia to a buyer in America.

With the proper intelligence we pin-pointed the time and place of the shipment. However, because we worked with INTERPOL, we could not pass classified government information to certain people without agreements, so we had to wait before we could act. The State Department was so difficult to work with during those years. They considered it an inconvenience to have someone review the information before we could share it.

It seemed to take forever, but once we finally got the approval, we moved immediately into position to rescue those girls. When we got there, we expected to find two eighteen wheelers carrying shipping containers with the girls. Unfortunately, because of the delay, we found only one. Half of the women we rescued from being delivered and the other half we lost. We do not know happened to them.

I thought all evening about the women we saved and the women we lost. I tried to imagine what it was like for them to be herded onto a shipping container in Asia then loaded onto a vessel for ocean travel. Those ships sometimes have anywhere from five hundred to seven hundred containers on them. Those girls had very little food and they were crowded together with no privacy. No matter if they screamed or banged on the side of the container it made no difference. No one was able to hear them.

Once they arrived at their port of debarkation, the container was placed on the back of a semi. From there they were trucked to their final destination. Their new lives as slaves began.

The thought of the plight of these young women terrorized my nights. It is still something I struggle with to this very day. On that occasion we saved fifty percent of the girls. That was better than the twenty percent we normally rescued, but it still felt like we failed.

When we opened the container, the girls were so scared. They figured they had reached their final destination and their life of slavery was about to begin. Several fought us trying to escape. It took hours trying to explain we were there to help them not to hurt them. I can only imagine what they went through on their voyage.

The anguish and mental havoc wreaked upon me was overwhelming. It was heartbreaking to fail. I knew these young women ended up in the hands of people who used them and tossed them aside like garbage in a waste basket. I far too often felt helpless. I spent many a night walking the floor pondering what I was doing and what more I could do.

★ ★ ★

My theme song in life was quickly becoming *"Rescue the Perishing."* In 2011, while traveling near Washington, DC, a car beside me was traveling in the HOV lane when I heard a tremendous boom. As I glanced to my left, I saw their front tire had blown out. Seconds later, the car banked sideways and flipped into the air, rolling over several times before coming to a stop right side up. The sight of this spinning, out of control vehicle was horrific. It was something you see in a movie, but this wasn't fiction, this was real life.

It amazed me people did not stop, they just drove right on by. My heart told me I could not do the same. I stopped my car and raced toward the accident. By the time I reached the vehicle, another man also arrived. He worked for the Secret Service. Together we did what we could to make the best out of a terrible situation. When I looked inside I could clearly see the driver was in shock. The passenger was in even worse condition. Blood was everywhere as bones where protruding out of his arms.

The Secret Service agent managed to get inside the car while I positioned myself near the head of the man. He was in such horrible condition. I could tell he also had a neck injury, so we carefully laid him back as we slowly removed him from the car. Once he was free from the accident we brought him over to the side of the road and laid him down. I kept my hands firmly on the side of his head and neck for the next twenty-five minutes until the Flight-for-Life chopper arrived. From all my years in the arena of paramedics and medicine I knew it was imperative we did not allow his head or neck to move. He was covered in blood and I became covered also, but despite the risks of an infectious disease, I did not let go. I kept his head and neck stable. I did not want to risk any chance of paralysis because of carelessness on my part.

Once the helicopter arrived, the paramedics successfully stabilized his body and flew him off to Fairfax County Medical Center where he received emergency trauma treatment. I don't know how he fared after that, but I pray all went well.

I don't know if I was always in the right place at the right time or the wrong place at the wrong time, I guess it depends on your perspective, but I do know I was constantly placed in situations where I played the role of rescuer.

On another occasion, my wife and I were traveling in Brooklyn when a man was crossing the street in front of us. Carefully we slowed down so he could cross but from out of nowhere a car came screaming down the street at breakneck speed. The man did not have a chance to even attempt to get out of the way. The car struck him going about forty-five miles per hour. The sound the body made against the metal was sickening.

The momentum from the vehicle launched the man through the air where he turned end over end until his body came crashing to the ground wedged beneath a parked car. My wife gasped in horror as the event transpired. Frozen in utter disgust, she could not move. I told her to sit still as I exited our vehicle and raced over to the man.

I tried to do what I could to free him but it was no use. The car had him pinned. I would definitely need help. Thankfully only seconds later another man showed up; a very big man. He was just what the doctor ordered.

I have read stories about people who have exhibited super human strength in life threatening situations, but I had never experienced it until then. This guy lifted the front of the car so I could remove the man.

He was wedged under so far the differential of the vehicle was laying on his chest preventing him from being able to breath. After I slid him out from under he was able to breathe on his own. We called 911 and the paramedics came to his assistance.

I made sure to thank the man with the cape and the big red S on his chest for his assistance. I know he was not really Superman and he did not have a cape or a big red S, but he did exhibit a feat of super human strength that was certainly something from out of this world.

All I have ever really wanted to do in life was help people, to rescue them or in essence to save them from the dangers lurking around every corner. I have had some successes and some failures, but I have always given my very best effort. Maybe my purpose in life is to be ready when called upon. That point became very clear to me on one special evening in February of 2015.

As they say on TV, the story you are about to hear is true, but the names have been changed to protect the innocent. That being said, this is an accurate chronicle of the events of that day.

I was out having dinner with my wife when I received a text from a former co-worker and friend of mine. We worked together at the Special Operations Command, so he knew my background and skillset very well. The text said, "You got a minute, I got something hot." Needless to say, my wife was none too happy I was reading text messages at dinner. However, from John I knew to take the message, because he never contacted me unless it was urgent. So I texted back, "Yes I am here."

John traveled from his home to Mississippi where he was visiting some friends. He was not there very long when Betty, an elderly neighbor lady came to the door knocking franticly. As soon as they opened the door, Betty began excitedly saying, "She is not here. She did not come today. She always comes, but she did not show up. Where is she? Where could she be? She always comes, she always comes, but she is not here."

As John listened, he knew something did not seem right. Her speaking was so frantic her sentences ran together so she barely made sense. John knew he needed more information, so he asked Betty, "What is the girl's name?" Betty could not remember.

John then asked, "What is her phone number?" Betty responded, "I don't know her number, she is always here. She should be here but she is not here. Where is she? Something must be wrong."

John could sense the despair in the lady's voice and his years of training told him she had a right to be fearful. John began to ask more questions, "Did she have a car? Did she take public transportation? What was the time she usually arrived? How long did she stay and when did she leave?" John made sure to diligently gather every piece of information he could to help assess the situation at hand.

This was the hot issue John texted me about. So, after I replied and told him I was available, he then asked, "What can you find out about this person?" He proceeded to text me the background information he gathered from Betty.

The missing lady was African American, somewhere around five feet eight inches tall, about one hundred twenty-five pounds, slim build with hair combed down to her shoulders. She always wore nail polish on her fingers but not on her toes. She usually wore open-toed shoes. She used public transportation to get to the residence and she always carried her frequent traveler card.

After sending me all that, he asked, "So can you do anything with that information and this address?" He then texted me the home address of Betty. I responded, "The lady we are trying to find, she doesn't live at this address?" He replied, "No, she does not." I was confused so I asked, "Why this address then?" John texted, "She is a caretaker for Betty." Now things were starting to make sense.

I texted back to him, "Okay, I can start with this." John was shocked, but glad at the same time. Immediately, I texted my son who was at home. I instructed Aaron to do a search on any medical service companies with Betty's address in their profile. We call this open source intelligence information gathering.

After a few minutes of investigation, his search returned one hit. We now had the name of a company. At the same time, John managed to get from Betty the cell phone number of the missing lady's brother. With this information I knew we had a solid lead.

Finding the owner of a cell phone can't be accomplished via normal Web searches. You have to go to the hacker pages to gather this data. Since my background is in the world of cyber intelligence I knew how to accomplish that feat.

Once I discovered the name of the brother was Richard, we began doing people searches for anyone associated to him. We combed all the social media sites and before long we found a girl who matched the description of the one missing who was associated to Richard. The girl's name was Nancy.

With all of that information, Aaron and I were able to determine Nancy's location. We found out she lived across town, right near the bus route. With the name and address in our possession, I sent the information back to John via text.

John immediately got into his car and began to drive to the neighborhood of the address where Nancy lived. He was very diligent in getting the lay of the land and where the bus picked up passengers in that area.

Since I spent pretty much the entire dinner on my phone texting, we decided to leave early and head for home. As soon as I arrived, I went to see what else Aaron had dug up. Immediately, I took the lead and worked behind the scenes, gathering more vital statistics and intelligence about the situation at hand. With my experience, I knew how to do more detailed searches and I hoped it would help us solve this mystery.

I contacted John by phone. He was out driving around looking for the home. The streets were poorly marked and he was having difficulty locating the residence. Aaron and I brought up a Google street view of the area and noticed a Goodwill store near where we believed the lady lived. From this map we were able to guide John to the correct location.

When John pulled onto the street he said, "Looks like this could be something. I see a couple of guys standing out in front of the house smoking cigarettes. One is on one side of the house and the other guy is on the other side. You can tell they are keeping watch. This does not look right."

I told him, "Well, call me back when you are done with your area canvas."

John parked his car, walked up to the house and began talking with one of the guys. He asked, "Is Nancy here?" The man responded, "No man, she isn't here." He proceeded to ask a few more questions, but the guys got very uncomfortable, so John decided he'd better leave.

Deep down, John knew the girl had probably been kidnapped, but the kidnappers were not very bright, because they brought her back to her own home and placed a couple guys as watch dogs outside.

John got into his car and drove up the block where he waited for about fifteen minutes. He then proceeded to drive back past the house. As he passed by he held up his cell phone so he could snap pictures of everything he could. He especially wanted to make sure that the men with whom he had spoken were clearly visible in the photos.

As soon as he got out of sight he immediately texted the photos to me. I was able to utilize facial recognition software and search through criminal databases until I had a match. Like I said, I am well versed in the world of cyber intelligence. I learned both guys had criminal records in the State of Mississippi.

Since I had their names, I quickly texted the information to John who then proceeded to drive back to the house. He got out of his car and walked straight up to the first man and called him by name. The man responded, "Bubba, who is Bubba?" John laughingly said, "You are Bubba and I also know that you have done time."

John then began to list all of his criminal record. Feeling very brazen John then asked, "Hey Bubba, aren't you on probation? If that is the case then why are you carrying a piece?" Bubba was none too happy, so he told John it was time for him to move on.

As John left the yard the guys were so unnerved they both went inside the house. John knew he was on to something and I knew we must do everything we could to rescue the girl. I did not want to go to bed yet another night having let someone's life slip through my hands.

John and I both knew we had the right house, we knew we had the right guys, so we deduced the girl must be inside. One other very valuable piece of data we uncovered was these guys supposedly had friends in the local police department. With that knowledge in hand, John decided to take all the information about the girl and the situation directly to the FBI. He felt this was the best option.

Kidnapping is actually the jurisdiction of the FBI anyway so it made sense for him to go to them first. With all the information he presented, they were able to go to a judge and get a warrant to search the house for the missing girl.

From John's first text to me until the time they had the warrant from the judge it had been just a little over four hours. That was extremely good.

Now, it was simply a waiting game. I had no clue when the FBI would go in, but I knew I did everything I could to save that woman's life.

Twenty-four hours passed and the FBI were yet to act. From what John told me, there was something stopping the raid. Then forty-eight hours passed and still nothing. It was driving me crazy, why were they risking this woman's life?

John and I spoke and he decided he would drive by Nancy's home once again. When he got to the house he saw Bubba and his buddy out on the front porch. They immediately reached for their guns, but John stepped on the gas and was out of reach before a shot could be fired.

The next day John called me with bad news. He had been by the house and everyone was gone. No one was there. They cleared out. John's words were heartbreaking to me, "I am sorry Peter, but it looks like we lost her." I was devastated. Once again I failed to rescue.

A deep gloom of depression permeated my entire countenance for about three hours until I received a text message from John. In his message was a link to an online news article. I clicked the link and began to read the words that changed my day.

The story told about a lady who was found in the parking lot of Lowes. The lady was Nancy. Her hands were bound behind her back with duct tape around her throat. She managed to get away from her captors and fled through the nearby woods to the Lowes parking lot.

One of the customers heading back to his car saw the girl unclothed and partially bound come across the parking lot. He immediately came to her rescue. My heart burst with joy as I read the article. She was not dead, she was alive.

We found out later Nancy was kidnapped from Wal-Mart by the brother and nephew of her landlord. When they snatched her they did not know that information. They just picked her out randomly from all the people in the store on that particular day.

Sure makes you realize the importance of concealed carry doesn't it?

Nancy was able to identify her kidnappers and they were arrested. They had kept her tied up in a tent behind the house John kept visiting. His numerous investigations provided her with the opportunity to escape. It goes to show that our efforts made a difference. I had not failed.

This whole incident as well as my whole life can best be summed up by the chorus of a popular song sung in churches all over the world. Funny how it is basically the same words the man of God shared with me all those many years ago. After all this time I finally understand, I do my part, and He does His.

Rescue the perishing,
Care for the dying,
Jesus is merciful,
*Jesus can save.**

One final note, so far, my mother has been wrong. I have never been shot. Let's just hope it stays that way.

---

*Rescue the Perishing, Frances J. Crosby, 1869

Star Spangled Banner Yet Wave

S hots fired from all directions as the enemy closed in. We did our best, but we were outnumbered. Everyone in my unit was killed except me and one other member. Surrounded by our adversary, we had no choice but to surrender. My existence as a front line infantry soldier was over; I was now a prisoner of the dreaded German SS troops. My next stop, a Nazi stalag. My name is Herman, but my friends call me Zerg and this is my story.

Few people really understand the cost of freedom or what it means to have it taken away. When I went off to war it was because Uncle Sam pointed a finger at me and said, "I need you." I was raised to be a patriot, one who loves and supports their country with an overwhelming trust in the providence of God.

I was born the fifth day of January, 1924, in a little town called Woodsfield in the great state of Ohio. Other than my time in the military, I have lived there my entire life.

We lived across from the local jail and courthouse about half a block from the main square of town. My dad had a garage, a repair shop, and a gas station just behind the post office. He worked hard and always provided for our family. He taught me the principles of what it takes to be a man.

It was a quiet existence but all that changed the day the Japanese attacked Pearl Harbor. Many of my father's customers and our friends were either drafted or volunteered to enter the military. It was just a given we were going to fight for our freedom. No one I knew ever thought about leaving the country or giving in to terrorism.

I was in high school when the attack on our nation occurred, but I knew as soon as I graduated what I wanted to do. I was going to serve my country. I was going to fight for freedom. They did not need to draft me, I willingly volunteered.

I remember where I was when I found out about the bombing of Pearl Harbor. My friend and I had gone to the matinee at the local movie house. When we came out of the theatre, Glenn and Molly, who owned the place, called us both over and told us about the attack. I was seventeen years old and a senior in high school, but I knew my destiny would be the war.

I enlisted right after I graduated and it was not long before I headed off for training. I was amazed at the number of people who came to see us off. Since it was a small town I knew most people in the area as well as most in the county. The folks really showed appreciation to us boys who were about to become fighting men.

We left Woodsfield and headed to Clarksburg, West Virginia for our exam. I was surprised they made me the acting corporal for those thirty-seven draftees even though almost everyone was older than me. I passed my exam with flying colors; I was officially a soldier in Uncle Sam's Army. You never met someone more ready to serve his country.

In January of 1943, I left for basic training aboard a bus for Fort Hayes in Columbus, Ohio. They needed guys for the infantry and that suited me just fine, so I was sent to Camp Croft in South Carolina. This was where my training in earnest began. For the next seventeen weeks the Army did its best to turn this boy into a man.

After I completed my training, I was granted a seven day furlough so I could return home before heading to Hampton Roads, Virginia. I was excited to see my family, but the visit was very short.

No one said it, but I knew they wondered if they would ever see me again. I wondered the very same thing.

I left the United States for Salerno Bay, Italy as a member of the 36th Infantry Division. I was in the 3rd squad, 3rd platoon of the 141st regiment. We were the first American division to invade the European mainland and test the defenses of Hitler's war machine.

I had always heard wonderful things about Italy as a child, but what we experienced was anything but beautiful. The number of causalities was astronomical. Every battle demanded a determination to live.

The Germans had a clear defensive line across the mountains of Mt. Camino, Mt. Maggiore, and Mt. Lungo. Breaking through would prove to be quite difficult, but it was our assignment. We needed desperately to overtake San Pietro and secure an American foothold in Hitler's Europe.

The Germans held the high ground, so the task at hand would not be an easy one. Our initial assault was stopped dead in its tracks. We suffered heavy losses due to mines, automatic weapons crossfire, and mortars reigning down upon us. The weather was horrible, a nasty combination of rain, cold, mud, and wind.

Those conditions went on for months. We were fighting a battle against an enemy with a fortified position and we were a group of soldiers who had very little food, water or sleep. Needless to say, our spirits were mighty low, but our resolve was still high. We knew we had to win this battle, losing was not an option.

Around the middle of December, we were ordered once again to make an all-out attack on the German position. This time, the outcome was different as we penetrated through the German defenses. The automatic weapons firing upon us killed several of the guys in my unit. By the grace of God, I was spared.

It was a costly battle, but we finally made our way to San Pietro. The next day, the Germans counterattacked, trying to retake the town, but a coordinated divisional strike finally secured the place for us. Of the sixteen tanks we used for the battle, only four remained. More than eleven hundred men were lost from my regiment alone. War is never a good thing, but sometimes it is a necessary one.

The Germans terrorized that poor town. When a woman innocently stepped foot out of her home to get water, a German sniper would pick her off from a hidden location. It was sad to see a young family lose their mother. I was thrilled we were able to free these people from Nazi tyranny.

Christmas of 1943 came and went with me on the battlefield. By the time the New Year rolled over we were still trying to gain control of the Liri Valley. We knew this was an important route to Rome.

Things turned ugly for the 36th when on January 20th of 1944 we were ordered to cross the rain-swollen Rapido River. As we piled weapons, soldiers, and ammunitions into our rubber boats I had a feeling we were going to be sitting ducks. My thoughts were spot on.

The Germans were waiting for us with small arms, machine guns, mortars, and tanks. Our assault went wrong from the very start. German mines and troops ripped our soldiers to shreds. A few of my unit managed to cross the river, but there were too few of them to make any difference. By the time the failed assault was over, more than twenty one hundred men of the 36th were either dead or reported missing.

The bodies of my friends were the ones who swam the cold Rapido River on that dreadful night. They fell under a barrage of mortar and automatic weapon fire. They faithfully followed orders, but they did not have a chance to succeed. From the beginning, the plan was destined to be a failure. When it was all over, the color of the Rapido ran red with the blood of American soldiers. I am truly thankful to still be alive.

If you travel to that area of Italy today, you will see tucked in a corner near San Angelo a monument dedicated to the 36th. It reads, "Trusting in God, they fought and died for liberty." If it weren't for our trust in God, many of us would never have returned.

The scene at the Rapido River will be forever seared into my mind. There were parts of bodies lying everywhere and cries for a medic echoed across the cold body of water but no medic would ever arrive; they too were killed. It was a very dark day. I wish I never experienced such a horrible event.

★ ★ ★

For the next several months, my unit continued to fight the battles of war. The Anzio Beachhead was our next major operation. I was dumped in water waist deep with my rifle held above my head while shots were firing all around. It was brutal.

The battle became a four month stalemate with a terrible casualty rate. The Germans had a huge piece of artillery called the "Anzio Annie." It was mounted on a flat rail car and they fired it once a day before hiding it in a tunnel. The devastation it brought was unbelievable.

The Nazi's were ruthless. They fired at hospitals, killed medics, and shot innocent civilians. Nothing was sacred to them. From our initial landing in January until our breakthrough in June we experienced a terrible beating. We had to fight no matter how bad the odds. The water was behind us, we had nowhere to fall back.

When we finally broke through we knew our next destination would be Rome. I can remember quite well the day we entered the streets of that historic city. As we marched through the town, the citizens gave us a rousing reception. We even went to Vatican City and saw the pope. It was quite a momentous occasion.

The date was June 5th, 1944 and none of us knew what was about to occur on the coast of France; D-Day was waiting in the wings. As I look back I feel our invasion and success in Italy gave Allied troops the time and support they needed for the Normandy invasion.

After Rome we prepared for the invasion of Southern France. I remember the day we landed. Our mission was to seal off the German Nineteenth Army. By the seventh day we penetrated some two hundred fifty miles into the country, but from there the fighting would get tough. Where we were once moving the distance of miles it was down to in yards. The next several months were hard on us all.

Christmas of 1944 came and I was still on the battlefield, but Uncle Sam gave us some relief from the fighting. We were in continuous combat for one hundred thirty-two days. Needless to say, a break to celebrate the birth of the Savior was a welcomed relief. As we marched through the town of Strasbourg, people came out onto the street to greet us. The townsfolk invited us to their midnight mass. I graciously accepted. It was so nice to be in a place with no war and death. The worship of the King of Kings was magnified greatly in my heart.

I could not speak their language, but when I heard the familiar tunes of Silent Night and Hark the Herald Angels Sing I felt at peace. It was quite an experience. It was my second Christmas away from home, but I felt just as close to the Lord there as I did in my own living room with my family.

The rest was brief, but it was enjoyed. The next stop for this rag-tag group of fighting men was Bitche, France. It turned out to be the southern end of the Battle of the Bulge. It was a time of desperation and despair.

The winter was brutally cold with the snow hip deep to most of us. Just maneuvering through the snow drifts was excruciating. I remember being so cold my feet were frozen and my hands were numb. To this day the winter cold still affects my feet and hands.

The fighting was hard. Three or four machine guns were blasting the snow all around. Areas once white were blood red. If the cold and enemy were not bad enough, we reached a part of France where several of the folks were sympathetic to the Nazis. It made every day a cold blooded fight for survival.

January continued to be cold and we fought several battles every day. I felt for sure it could not get any worse, but I was sorely mistaken. Everything changed on February 3rd, 1945. It was a day I will never forget.

★ ★ ★

The Rhine Valley lays about fifteen miles north of Strasbourg. It was there my life took a drastic turn. It was a lesson far too expensive for me to ever forget.

Our unit was ordered to make an attack on Herrlisheim. It was a brutally cold February morning when we began wading through the Zorn River. The water was swift moving and up to our chests. I held my weapon high above my head so it would not get wet. I could not take any risk of my rifle not firing when I needed it most.

My body ached with intense pain, but that did not matter, I had to push through my circumstances and get to the other side. When I reached the shore, I was welcomed with the sound of German automatic machine gun fire. Our tank support never arrived, but the Germans had their tanks in range and ready. Our casualty rate began to mount fast.

The mission was quickly failing, so orders were given for us to withdraw. Unfortunately those commands came far too late. From up in a church tower in the top of the steeple, the Germans had snipers who were taking out my fellow soldiers one by one.

Immediately, my platoon leader Joe Parks and I made a dash for cover. The nearest place of protection was a nearby ditch. It looked more like a long foxhole, but we did not care

We dove into the trench as shots landed around us. The taste of dirt filled my mouth as I hit the bottom of the hole. I grabbed my Thompson sub-machine gun and began to fire in every direction hoping to hit one of those snipers.

I was only twenty-one years old and my life was flashing before my eyes. I could see the Nazi SS troops slowly closing in around us. I had been fighting for weeks straight with no rest. I had not showered in three months and it looked like I was about to be killed by Hitler's elite fighting force.

Joe slowly rose to see how close they were when a shot went through his shoulder. He collapsed at my side writhing in pain and bleeding profusely. The SS were forming a circle around our position. Things were not good. I knew only one of two things could happen. I would either be killed or captured. Both were terrible options.

I knew if we were captured they would search us and there was only one item on me I did not want to lose. It was a wrist watch my parents purchased for me. It meant so much, so I hid it in my boot all the way down by the toe.

With nowhere to go and nothing we could do we slowly dropped our weapons and surrendered. I was dying inside at the thought of losing, but I was also worried about Joe. I prayed to God he would survive.

As we stepped out of the trench a tall, lanky SS officer searched me. Thankfully he did not find the watch. The only items I had on my person were seven chocolate bars. I never smoked or drank; chocolate was my vice of choice. In fact, when we got our rations I always traded my cigarettes for chocolate. To say I have a sweet tooth is a great understatement.

When the officer searched me, he found four of my candy bars in my left pocket, but he never searched the right so it left me three. You cannot imagine what that meant to me. In fact, on more than one occasion those pieces of chocolate helped to sustain my life.

I was ordered to walk to the train station, but I was not about to leave Joe behind to die so I carried him the entire way. He was losing so much blood, I feared for his life. When we finally reached the railroad station I laid him down inside on a long bench.

He was not doing well. Every breath took extra effort. The SS troops did not care at all about the situation; they kept sticking me with their bayonets trying to get me to move on. I was determined to stay by Joe's side. I begged one of the soldiers to please get a doctor;

I did not want to watch my friend die. Reluctantly, I agreed to leave and then I was taken away.

I looked back at Joe lying on the bench and prayed to God he would live. I had no way of knowing if I would ever see him again.

They marched me down to the edge of the Rhine River where they placed me with several other prisoners. We were taken across that body of water on a barge to a camp in Baden-Baden. Once we arrived, I was escorted into a large building where I was immediately thrown down into a damp dark dungeon.

When my body hit the floor I did not move. I was so physically and emotionally exhausted I just laid there. The feeling was horrific and all around I could hear terrifying noise. In fact, it was more than just a sound, it was several of them. I could feel the presence of something getting closer. My mind began to race as I felt the first wave of several creatures race across my back and head. I waved my arms hitting a few of them off me.

At first, I had no clue what I struck. When the next bunch of them came within range and began gnawing at my body I soon realized the dungeon was swarming with rats. These were no ordinary sized rodents; they were the size of house cats. I got to my feet and began to kick them off me. I was not about to lay there and become their dinner.

That rat-infested dungeon became my home. There was no bathroom, no place to sleep, and practically no food. Once a day, I was fed a bowl of grass soup. This was nothing more than a bunch of weeds the Germans pulled from the ground and cooked in a pot. Not only did it contain dirt and bugs, but the broth itself was even green. It was horrible, but it was the only food I received.

That is when those chocolate bars I had in my pocket became so valuable. Every day I took a very small, almost miniscule bite off one of the bars. I would let that chocolate just sit in my mouth and melt. I savored it for as long as I could before swallowing. Every ounce of sweetness was like honey from heaven.

The SS did not keep me there for very long. It was about four days later when I was transferred to Stuttgart before they re-located me to Stalag VII-A in Moosburg. That was a huge prisoner-of-war camp. It was originally meant to hold 10,000 prisoners, but I was told there were about 70,000 Allied soldiers held captive there.

Every day I was sure I was going to be executed by the German SS soldiers. It was a horrible existence. When rail cars rolled into the camp, the smell of human waste and dead bodies made us want to vomit. It was a stench you cannot even imagine.

Any day you knew you might be executed. On one occasion, a soldier pulled his gun, and placed it directly onto my head with the barrel directly between my eyes. He screamed at me, demanding I give him information about the Allied military plans. I calmly gave him the same answers as every other prisoner; name, rank, and serial number. He was so enraged, but he did not pull the trigger, instead I got the butt end of a rifle across my jaw.

The barracks in which we were housed were flea ridden and rat infested. We had no beds to sleep on, just slats of boards built on top of one another. It was like bunk beds without a mattress, box spring or pillow.

The SS soldiers always paid particular interest to me because of my name, it was of German ancestry. Every day I was interrogated. They demanded to know why someone who was German was fighting for the Allies. I may have been from German ancestry, but inside I was every bit a pure red-blooded American.

Every day I was hit, spat upon, kicked, and struck with the butt end of a rifle. This was bad enough but when they let the dogs loose on me it was horrific. The vicious biting teeth of those Nazi trained animals were bitter cruelty.

From Moosburg, I was transported to Munich. They took each of us and packed us into rail cars like we were herds of cattle. The smell was disgusting. There was no bathroom, no place to sit; you just stood there in filth. It was utter inhumanity.

As the train rumbled along we passed through town after town. People came out to the tracks and threw things at the rail cars or mocked us as we went by. There was no sign of compassion, just laughing torment. We were all freaks to the jeering crowd.

When we finally arrived in Munich we were immediately sent to work repairing the rail lines and yard. Allied bombers destroyed much of the infrastructure, so the Germans had us prisoners working to repair what was damaged.

It was bitter cold and we had no gloves. Every time I reached down to pick up a wooden railroad tie, it tore pieces of flesh from my hands. To this day my hands still bother me from that experience.

I really do not remember how long I was in Munich. The days all ran together. I never counted how long I was there, I was just amazed I survived. We were treated so savagely.

Every time the Allied soldiers came close, the Germans moved us to another camp. From Munich, I was transported once again by train to Markt-Pongau in Austria. This was by far the worst of the stalags for me. The entire camp was surrounded by razor sharp barbed wire. Soldiers with automatic weapons, dogs with vicious personalities, and the brutal cold made it no vacation spot.

The brutality of hunger tasked my senses. I had no solid food for months and my body was wasting away. I was down at around fifty pounds. The soup we were served once a day was made from garbage, dirt, weeds, and dandelions. The worms and bugs swimming in the soup were certainly no added bonus, but I ate them anyway, at least it was something solid.

Every day, we did our best to pick lice off one another. I had one shower the entire time I was imprisoned, but I had to put on the same flea infested clothes. We were subjected to forced labor twelve hours a day and if we fell out of step we were either bayoneted or shot. My skin became sore and irritated with no medical treatment offered to sooth my pain.

Dysentery tied my stomach into knots as I wondered how much longer I could endure such torment. I thought about my father and mother at home. Dad would most certainly be listening to the radio trying to find out anything he could about the war effort. Mom would be in the bedroom on her knees begging God to protect her son. Her prayers were most certainly answered.

I watched everyday as the vicious SS soldiers picked out a prisoner and beat him. My buddy, Jack, was brutally beaten to death and there was absolutely nothing I could do about it. It makes me sick to think about it.

The Germans tried to brainwash us into becoming Nazis. They tried every means necessary to get information, but it usually did not work. Our men were determined to stay Americans. We were not about to become a bunch of Benedict Arnolds.

At the prison camp, there were also several Russian prisoners who had been there from nearly the start of the war. They were very undernourished and looked pretty bad. A few of them could speak a little English so we communicated with them the best we could.

Occasionally, we were served some prison camp black bread. It was not much of a treat, but at least it was something to go with the soup. It was made from rye grain, sliced sugar beets, saw dust, minced leaves, and straw. It was not something you want to serve at your next dinner party.

Being a POW meant every day we hoped for a rescue. We prayed it would come, but we had our doubts. On more than one occasion, I wondered if I would ever make it out alive, but my spirits picked up when I began to see American bombers flying over our camp. We could hear the sounds of the explosions in the distance and every day they were getting closer. All we could do was pray and hope for the best.

Two mornings later, while standing out in the POW yard, a P51 fighter plane flew very low over the camp. We could see the pilot in the cockpit waving down at us. For the first time I noticed the

German soldiers looked fearful. It was almost like they knew their demise was at hand.

Every man in the camp began to anticipate the possibility of a rescue. Within an hour we heard the rumbling of tanks headed our way. When those armored beauties came crashing through the barbed wire, tears streamed down my face as I knew I was finally liberated.

On May 8th, 1945 when the 36th Texas regiment marched into that prison camp, the Nazi flag came down and the Stars and Stripes went up. I knew then the Star Spangled Banner still waved through-out the world, exclaiming there were men willing to risk their lives to save their fellow man. As we watched Old Glory fly, there was not a dry eye in the place. We stood at attention as tears streamed down our cheeks.

It turns out we were the last camp to be liberated during the war. I never received one package from the Red Cross. The Germans confiscated and withheld them from us. They wanted to make sure they could break our spirits. I am happy to say they never succeeded with me.

The rescuing officers gave us strict instructions to stay put. We were advised doctors and other medical professionals would arrive shortly to take care of us. We all faithfully followed the commands; however several of our Russian friends who were also captured did not listen and immediately headed into the nearby town.

That turned out to be a deadly mistake. When the Russians descended upon the town they found every bit of food they could eat and because of the intense hunger they experienced for so long, many began to gorge themselves. The stomach is a very thin muscle and it can only stretch so far. Since it shrunk so much because of their imprisonment, the excess food caused their stomachs to burst open, bringing forth a most miserable death. I can remember seeing some of them later lying near the camp. It was a gruesome sight to behold.

When the medical team arrived we were given very exacting instructions as to what we could eat. They started us out eating nothing but baby food. Then after a few days, small amounts of solid food were introduced back into our system. After I saw what happened to the Russians because of their overeating, I was determined to follow their instructions with strict care.

Within a few days, we were trucked to Salzburg, Austria where we were flown to the Allied Supreme Headquarters in Rheims, France. I remember getting to meet General Dwight D. Eisenhower. Days later we were transported to Le Havre where we boarded an English ship for America. On June 30th, we docked at Newport News, Virginia and as soon as my feet hit the ground I dropped to my knees and kissed the soil. I was never so glad to be back in America.

I knew exactly where my first stop would be. I immediately made my way down to the Post Exchange where I bought some chocolate bars and ice cream. It was time to feed my sweet tooth, which brought new meaning to the motto, "Home Sweet Home."

Many years passed after the war when one day I received a letter in the mail. It was from St. Louis, Missouri. When I opened the envelope, tears streamed down my face when I saw the signature. The letter was from Joe Parks, my former platoon leader who I was forced to leave behind on the bench in the train station. The Germans allowed a doctor to fix his shoulder. He also survived a stint in a prisoner-of-war camp.

We were both liberated by American troops who gave everything they had to rescue those in need. Many have called us the "Greatest Generation," I don't know for certain if that is true, but I do know this for sure. We were the generation who was willing to place our bodies, souls, and spirits into the hands of the Great I AM so we could fight the evils of Nazi tyranny in a world turned upside down.

America, please always remember this: Freedom is not free!

O'er the Land of the Free

My nervous mother sat in the small café. She was seventeen years old and seven months pregnant. The clock on the wall behind the counter told her something was very wrong. My father excused himself to go to the restroom, but that was more than thirty minutes earlier. Scared, alone, and very worried she politely asked the manager if he would walk back to see if everything was okay. The minutes he was away seemed liked hours. Finally, he returned with news and it was not good. My father was nowhere to be found, the bathroom window was open and his car was no longer in the parking lot. The hell that became my life had already begun and I had not even entered the world. My name is Erik and this is my story.

My mother was just a young girl of seventeen when she moved to East Los Angeles. She was all alone in the big city with nowhere to sleep and nowhere to work. It was not the best of situations, but she managed to land a job in a dry cleaning establishment. It seemed like she had finally caught a break, but perception was certainly not reality. In those days, the dry cleaning world was a popular place for gangsters to frequent. Being young and naïve, my mother became an easy target for one such individual in particular.

His words were smooth, his compliments were cunning, and his mannerisms swept my mother off her feet. Soft words soon turned to intimate romance. Within a few short months, my mother discovered she was with child; she was carrying a boy. She was a single, teenage girl in the city, pregnant with the baby of a gangster. I was that baby.

This situation was certainly not an ideal one. Yet my mother was excited, but my biological father seemed to have other ideas. The idea of being a daddy did not suit his lifestyle, so one day out of the blue he decided it would be fun if he and my mother took a trip down to Mexico.

Since it was close to the time of my birth, he told my mother it would be great if they could get away for some time alone. Being a soon-to-be mother the prospect of a getaway was very appealing so she enthusiastically said "Yes."

They made the long trip by car from Los Angeles to Sinaloa, Mexico. It was an arduous journey, but my mother did not care, because she was in love and had a new baby on the way. Everything seemed right in the world to her. Unbeknownst to my mother, the area where my father was taking her was a town known to be a stronghold for several drug cartels. She was innocent, naïve, and being taken for a ride.

Nothing seemed out of the ordinary, the day was one of fun and enjoyment when they stopped for something to eat at a casual little café in the city. They had not been in the restaurant for very long before my father excused himself to go to the restroom. My mother patiently waited at the table looking over the menu. The choices all looked very appealing because she was quite hungry. However, before long she began to grow anxious as she sat there alone. Something did not seem right; he was gone for far too long.

Nervously, my mother asked one of the waiters if someone could go see if everything was okay in the men's restroom. She explained that her boyfriend had been in the bathroom for almost thirty minutes and she was worried. The waiter nodded, and then headed off to speak to the manager so he could handle her request.

Her fear turned into a living nightmare when the manager spoke the words she did not expect to hear. "I am sorry miss, but he is not in there. He is gone, the window is open. I am afraid it looks as if you have been abandoned."

My mother quickly stood up and raced out into the parking lot only to see her worst fears confirmed. The car was gone, she had been left behind. Broken hearted, she fell to the ground and sobbed uncontrollably. Her heart was broken, her life was destroyed, and her baby would be born without his father.

Alone, rejected, and afraid my mother knew she had no way to get back to Los Angeles. Her only option was to find a way to survive until she could return to the United States. Fortunately, she did have an aunt who lived in Mexico, but the journey to her house would not be an easy one for anybody, let alone a seventeen year-old girl who was more than seven months pregnant, and with no money. However, she managed to get there and within a month and a half I entered the world, frail and unhealthy. I would not eat. In fact, they had to place intravenous tubes in my sick little body just to keep me alive.

After a couple of days, she was informed by the doctors that unless I could get consistent medical treatment I would most likely not live. It was at this point my mother knew she must do whatever was necessary to get herself and her baby boy back to Los Angeles. She was determined to make it or we would both die trying.

Thankfully for us, my mother befriended a girl who agreed to help her get back to America. During this time period it was quite easy to cross the border from Mexico into the U.S. When they reached the border at Tijuana, the guard asked for my mother's friend's credentials. She showed him her driver's license and birth certificate and said, "My cousin and I have been on vacation, we are looking forward to getting home." The guard just motioned them through.

He never asked for anything from my mother, nor did he ask to see what was in the ice chest in the back seat. Had he looked in there, he would have found me. I made my first trip to America in an igloo ice container. First class accommodations all the way.

I really don't know how she did it, but she managed to get me to the UCLA medical center. Had she not succeeded, the story of my life would be much shorter. She knew the cost would be high, but she was determined to find a way to pay for my treatment.

She was able to return to the dry cleaners for work once again. Every day, she worked all day long and then she came to visit me. It was difficult, but her determination and her love for me made all the difference in the world. Too bad things didn't stay that way.

I am sure it was a multitude of factors that caused the stress, but my mother began to have mental issues and unfortunately she would take them out on me. The beatings I endured should never happen to anyone, let alone a seven month old baby, but they did. Of course I don't remember them, but family and friends who witnessed the assaults said they were quite disturbing. It was not uncommon for me to have bruises all over my small face and body.

The direction of my life went from bad to worse when my mother met a new man. Unfortunately for me, my mother decided to marry him. I had a new dad. However, nothing about him represented the attributes of the term father. The beatings I received from my mother were child's play compared to what he delivered.

It is so hard to explain what I experienced. Up until the time I was fifteen-years-old I believed he was my father. I did not know I had a biological dad who abandoned me. Abuse of one fashion or another occurred every day and I had no clue why. It was just something I grew to expect.

I received my first broken nose by him at the age of five. During the 1970s we never wore seatbelts when riding in a car, my mother just held me on her lap. On one occasion, they got into a heated argument and I received the brunt of the disagreement. While he was driving he yelled at my mother and said, "I know how to make you shut up," and with those words he back-handed me with a fist right in the nose. Blood flew everywhere as the small bridge of my nose was shattered. I screamed in pain before being hit again and told to shut up. That is what I lived with on a regular basis.

Despite the abuse and hatred I endured, I loved him and my mother so much. I could not fathom what I had done to receive their hostility and abuse. I was just a small boy desperately seeking the love of his parents and finding none.

During those early years of my life, my mother became pregnant several more times. As I gained new brothers and sisters, I soon realized I was the main target for the beatings. I was constantly singled out from amongst the others.

It is a terrible feeling to realize you are unwanted. I was not allowed to have seconds on food unless everyone else was finished eating all they wanted. I was definitely the black sheep of the family. My parents stole my smile. I walked around all the time with a frown on my face. I just could not understand why I was being treated so poorly in my own home. It was devastating.

As I got older I found myself staying with different aunts every week, because my step-father did not want me around and my mother went along with everything he said. I had no stable home life whatsoever.

In the entirety of my childhood I had just two birthday parties. In fact, I can recall only one time my mother said she loved me. It was a very sad and lonely existence.

With my teenage years about to arrive, I began spending a lot of time in the local gym, learning how to box. Not only had I become a good fighter, but I also proved to be skilled on the soccer field. The boxing gym and the soccer stadium became my new homes, because I had friends there who listened and cared about me. Well I thought that then, but now I know better.

At the age of thirteen I joined a new family when I and a few friends from the gym were initiated into the VNE. The VNE stands for Varrio Nueva Estrada. They are a Chicano street gang founded in the Boyle Heights area of California. It is one of the most prominent and deadly street gangs in East Los Angeles. They are one of thirty-four gangs located in a fifteen square mile area of the city.

Looking back, I know it was stupid to join them, but when you are young and looking for somewhere to belong, it seemed like the best option. For the most part it seemed to me to be the only option.

Joining a gang is not like joining a local club. You get *jumped* into them which means they test to see if you have heart. I was attacked by six or seven guys older than me. I basically had to fight all of them for a specified time frame. They do this to see if you can hold your own.

When you live in a gang infested area you have to watch your back every day. When you go across the street to get eggs or milk you can expect to either get beat up, stabbed, or shot. It is a life where you must constantly be vigilant and aware.

Not only were you tested for heart, but the gang also wanted to make sure you were not a "ranker." A ranker is someone who gets asked from another gang what hood you are from and the "ranker" will not say anything because they are afraid of possibly getting beaten or worse. The VNE wanted no rankers in their midst. If they determined you had this character trait it was not a good thing. They would come after you or your family. It usually ended in a death sentence.

By joining VNE my whole life changed and it was not for the good. I was taught very quickly how to do a host of criminal activities. I can still remember being instructed in the art of doing a walk or drive by shooting. "It should be quick and effective," they told me, "If you are good, then they will be dead or at least they will not mess with the VNE ever again." These were certainly not good life lessons for a thirteen-year-old.

It was important for us to make sure only members of our gang were in VNE territory. If we noticed someone we did not recognize we walked right up to them and asked, "Who you with?" If we found out they were from a rival gang, we would either stab or shoot them. We had to send the message this was VNE turf and we do not take trespassing lightly.

Extortion, racketeering, money laundering, theft, murder, drugs, you name the crime and we were involved in it. It was all about getting money. My cousin and I joined VNE at about the same time. We wanted to be part of a family. The gang brought us acceptance, but it came at a high cost. In fact, my cousin is still in prison today. He has been there for more than twenty-three years.

I liked the getting money aspect of being a gangster. It made me feel like I was an entrepreneur. I loved coming up with creative ways to extract money from people. Gang banging was just part of the business I had to do in order to be successful. It was a warped way of thinking, but to a young teenager it all made sense.

One night when I was thirteen, my friend and I waited outside a Mexican bar for it to close. As the druggies came out the door in their intoxicated states, they were easy prey for us. In the darkness we waited for the opportunity to spring into action. You could hear the screams and commotion as we attacked them with knives and clubs. I remember well swinging and taking out their knees while my friend stabbed them. They never saw it coming. As they laid on the street bleeding and half unconscious, we took everything of value. Their boots, belt buckles, gold chains, and money provided our bounty for the evening exercise. We were modern day pirates looting the asphalt seas of Los Angeles.

Crime became a fine science of observation. We would stake out an area all day long and simply watch what people did. It did not take very long to see their patterns develop. We utilized this information to steal their cars and rob their homes while they were away.

That was easy money, but the risks certainly were high. It did not take me long to realize I had to find a better way to make money. The answer soon presented itself in the selling of drugs.

That was a business opportunity right up my alley. People addicted to drugs were everywhere I turned, so it was easy for me to feed that addiction. Those who were hooked the worst would pay any amount just to satisfy their craving for a brief window of time.

Every time I sold a score I carefully observed what happened to the folks who bought my drugs. Their lives were a mess, but I did not care. I only wanted their money, but in this experience I did learn a valuable lesson. I knew if I did not use drugs I could be very successful, so from that day forward I determined to be the dealer and not the doer.

I became quite adept at taking high quality cocaine, cutting it down, and reselling the diluted product for the same price as the original grade. I was so good many could not tell the difference. It was easy money. I was gaining power and influence at the tender age of fourteen.

Before long, my abilities began to be noticed by a group called La eMe, also known as the Mexican Mafia. This group is the controlling organization for almost every Hispanic gang in Southern California. They have a very strict set of rules in their constitution and membership is by invitation only. You don't go to them, they come to you.

After my cousin and I became members of La eMe, it was not uncommon for a senior member to give us instructions for a task they wanted executed. This usually meant a hit on someone. I would go and recruit about five people or soldiers as we called them, to come with me. These would all be guys who wanted to be in the Mexican Mafia. So to prove their allegiance they would have to carry out the hit. That would be a testament of their worth to the organization.

I saw guys get their heads blown off. I watched hits go down with murderous precision. Look at your thirteen and fourteen-year-old children and think about them leading a group of wannabe hit men to a rendezvous with horrific intentions. I was that child. I had guidance, but it was not the kind any child should ever receive. I still have nightmares today about the warm blood running down over my hand from a stabbing in which I participated.

That was my entire life for the next two and a half years; a gang-banging, drug dealing terror on the streets of East Los Angeles. I had money, power, and prestige in my territory. I was also becoming well versed in the art of street fighting. It did not matter the size of the individual in front of me, I learned how to take people out with cunning precision few adults possess, let alone a teenager.

It got to the point where rival gangs would send people much bigger and older onto my turf. Their mission was to take me out. On one occasion, it almost came to fruition when I was met in the street by a guy much larger than me and twenty-two years my senior. I could tell by looking into his face why he was there. I knew this was not going to end well. Within minutes he was pummeling my body with lefts and rights. No matter where I hit him, it did not phase this monster of a man.

As I tried to strike him across the neck he kicked me severely in the groin, sending me to the ground. Then I saw it appear, a twelve inch knife with a blade of steel reflecting the noon day sun. As he went to stab me I tried to slide away but he got part of my side. I felt the blade rip off a sliver of my flesh. Feeling my warm blood run down my side enraged me to the point I sprung up from the ground and charged the guy. The force of me hitting his body sent the knife flying as we both crashed to the ground.

The fight did not last as bystanders began to break up the struggle. I was bleeding, dirty, and mad, but I did not care. I was still alive and figured I would have another chance to get even one day.

After that fight, I began to feel I was unbeatable and for the most part things for me were going along great. I controlled a territory where I ran my operation and I had plenty of money to do what I wanted. In my warped mind, everything in my life was perfect, until the day came when I met the man in the blue uniform.

★ ★ ★

It was a typical Saturday night for me as a sixteen-year-old street thug. I was cruising the streets in my decked out Cutlass Supreme with the fancy rims and loud music. I loved that car and I drove it everywhere. It did not matter to me I had no driver's license. I was above the law and I operated on my own rules. I had plans for a big night, but that changed when I saw a black and white unit with his lights on in my rearview mirror. Immediately, I let out a string of expletives as I eased my car over to the curb. In my mind I did not need to be hassled by this cop and I was going to do my best to play it cool.

As the officer reached the window he looked at me and said, "Where are you going little Homie?" I said nothing and just kind of pointed in a direction. The officer saw my uneasiness and told me to step out of the car. I knew things were about to go from bad to worse. After a few minutes of inspection the officer hit the jackpot when he uncovered a treasure trove of illegal contraband.

I originally planned to spend the night taking my stash of cocaine and cutting it with baking soda to quadruple the amount. There were numerous ways to increase the supply which in return increased my profits. The night would play out much differently than planned.

It took only a few moments for the officer to confiscate my drugs, my car, and the six thousand dollars in cash I was carrying. I often had large sums of money with me. In fact, the thing I loved about the drug business was the amount of revenue I collected. I saw on the streets an endless supply of dollar bills waiting to be extracted from suckers who were addicted. It's like a powerful politician overtaxing a gullible public who begs you to do more.

I just knew I was about to be arrested, but that did not happen. Instead, he gave me a card with his name and phone number on it and told me to beat it. However, before I left he turned and said, "Hey, give me a call sometime."

Needless to say, I knew this was not normal and my mind pondered the incident as I began to make the long treacherous walk back to East L.A. This would not be easy because I was on the other side of the city. It took me hours to sneak through other gang infested neighborhoods without being noticed. I knew if I got caught in their territory it would be a death sentence or at the least a trip to the emergency room.

I was so angry at the officer because he took everything from me, but I had his card and I couldn't help but wonder why he gave it to me. After about a week I decided I would call him. I had to determine what was his angle?

My anxiety intensified as I dialed his number. When he answered the phone I kind of mumbled my name and asked, "Do you remember me?" He replied, "Yeah, I remember you. So, do you want to meet?" Questions ran recklessly around my head as I pondered, "What could this guy want?" I asked him why he wanted to meet and he stated we should get together for lunch sometime. Reluctantly, I agreed to a place and time.

The apprehension I felt as I walked to the little chicken restaurant was overwhelming. I was a sixteen-year-old street thug living a life of evil, walking to have lunch with an officer. Things just didn't add up, but curiosity took over my thought process. I had to know what he wanted.

When I walked in, I saw him sitting at a table in the corner. I carefully sauntered over and took a chair across from him. It did not take him long to make his intentions clear. "So little Homie, you want to do business with me?" I paused, not sure what to say. My mind raced in a hundred different directions. Was this a setup? Was he trying to infiltrate the gang? What did he hope to gain? I straight out asked him, "What kind of business?"

The officer began to methodically lay out his scheme, "Here is what I can do. Just like I pulled you over and took all your stuff, I can do the same thing to others. We can then designate a place to meet and

I will sell those items to you and you can then sell them to others. It is a win-win situation for us both. So, what do you say, are you game?"

I could not believe what I was hearing, but due to my corrupt way of thinking I was open to the business proposition. I looked him in the eye, smiled and agreed to the arrangement. A new sense of power began to percolate through my mind. With a cop on my side I would be untouchable.

Anytime I could find new sources of revenue, I was all for it. To remain a member of the Mexican Mafia, it cost me five thousand dollars a month. Once you are in the gang you have to pay to retain the right to be a "thirteen." That is what we are, "thirteens." The letter M is the thirteenth letter of the alphabet and that is the mark of the Mexican Mafia. Since I needed the money, it was an easy decision to partner with this crooked cop.

The first time we met it was a good haul for me. I made out quite well in the exchange. We met a couple more times, but by the time the fourth meeting rolled around I began to feel very uneasy about the situation. Something did not seem right.

Even though I felt uneasy, I agreed to meet with him at his home. When I entered the house we went to the kitchen and sat down at the table. Everything felt wrong. I had this sense he was out to get me. After a few minutes I said, "I am going to get a drink of water." I got up and walked past the officer to the sink located behind him. I turned on the faucet, however, this was just for a diversion. I turned back around pulling out my .32 revolver. I was determined to make sure I walked out of there alive. I quickly reached across his shoulder and shoved my weapon into his chest area. Before he could say a word I pulled the trigger three times. He slumped over in his chair onto the table.

With the officer out of the way I began to make my way through the house taking everything of value I felt was rightfully mine. I took all the drugs, money, and weapons I could find. As soon as I had everything I wanted, I left.

I figured this would be an easy get away, but I was certainly wrong on that account. What I did not know was the officer was under surveillance, because folks in his precinct knew he was crooked. As soon as I made my way out of the house and into the car, they immediately had units on my tail.

While I was cruising down the road I kept noticing a helicopter above my car. It seemed strange to me at the time, I had no clue where they could be going flying so close to the ground. It was no matter to me, I had my tunes, my money, and my drugs. My enemy was out of the way and I had nothing but clear sailing ahead. However, when I pulled into the apartments where I lived, I soon found a different story. Within seconds another helicopter was on the scene and landed nearby. SWAT teams swarmed the area and shouts rang out, "Stop, get out of the car now and put your hands on your head." Cops were everywhere. Sharp shooters were scattered all over the apartments, trained on my every move. They had me, I had nowhere to go.

I knew I was busted, but one thing I did not know was the condition of the officer I shot three times. I just assumed I killed him, but what I did not know at the time was he was wearing his bullet proof vest. My shots did considerable damage, but not enough to take his life. When I left his house it was not long before he was found by the local authorities. They rushed him to the hospital where he remained in a coma for several weeks. Even though he was shot point blank range, amazingly, he survived.

I of course did not know that when I was taken down to the station. Regardless of what they had on me, I was determined to beat the system. Once I arrived, I was questioned relentlessly about my relationship with the officer. They asked me who shot him and I told them I did not know. I lied and said there were other guys around the table also but I did not know who they were. I was lying through my teeth trying to get out of the mess I made. There was no denying it, I was in serious trouble and was getting what I rightfully deserved.

I was making one terrible decision after another in my life. I had become pure evil walking the streets of East L.A. The whole time it was happening I could not see it, but now it is easy for me to realize just how wicked I had become. My life started badly and now it was going to get worse. However, I really had no one to blame but myself, I may have been dealt a bad hand, but I was the one making all the wrong choices.

My incarceration began at the local juvenile detention center while I waited for my trial. Word quickly got around that I shot a cop and because of this fact I became the big man on campus you might say. I was already a young man with a lot of street cred, but this act upped me in the rankings.

My case would never come to trial because I made a deal with the prosecuting attorney. This was all made possible because I was able to purchase a very good lawyer. The years I spent selling drugs provided for me a huge sum of money. I was able to use that to acquire one of the best defense attorneys in the area.

He managed to get my sentence down to about ten years. Since the police officer did not die, I was not tried for murder, but I did end up getting saddled with two felonies. The prosecuting attorney figured that once I got out I would mess up again and then they could get a life sentence on me. I would say in most circumstances that definitely works out to be the situation.

I spent my first little bit of time behind bars at the California Youth Authority. The facility is supposed to provide training, treatment, and education services to the most serious juvenile offenders. That might be the case, but I was not there very long because I was kicked out of the program for being a problem. From there they sent me to the California Correctional Institution at Tehachapi.

While there, I hired another lawyer to fight to have my sentencing changed from adult to juvenile. This was crucial to me on two important levels. On the first level, I knew the time served would most likely be less and secondly if I could stay out of trouble I would get out of prison with a clean record.

Staying out of trouble proved not to be an easy task. I once again had to be transferred because of my behavior. From Tehachapi I went to Salinas Valley and then on to the California State Prison at Corcoran. That was a level four facility which housed the worst of the worst.

Surviving in prison for me was really no big deal. It was not long before I set up my own drug running business from inside the facility. I had people from the outside smuggling cocaine and heroin to me. My high school girlfriend was my biggest asset in that endeavor. Every time she came to visit she hid small pieces of rock cocaine or heroin somewhere on her person.

When she arrived at the facility I was taken to a small area where we could be alone for a conjugal visit. Once there, getting the drugs from her was no problem. The real issue was smuggling them back into the cell block. There were numerous ways to do this, but my preferred method was to swallow a small balloon with the drugs contained inside. Once I got back in my cell I would make myself throw up. The balloon containing the drugs could then be easily retrieved from my vomit.

I knew I had just a brief amount of time to execute that technique. It takes about forty-five minutes for a balloon to traverse its way through the human body. If I waited too long, I missed the opportunity to retrieve it by throwing up. This meant I would have to wait until I went to the bathroom and get it from there.

Drugs reap big dividends when you are in prison. Inmates knew they could score a hit from me, but it would cost them. I was able to extract all kinds of favors and privileges from not only fellow prisoners, but also from guards. Even being incarcerated did not prevent me from living a life of power and control. My stock and credibility were rising in the criminal world.

In fact, ever since I was about twelve-years-old, my goal was to go to prison. I know this is a foreign concept to many, but for me I knew the prestige it would bring in the world of the streets. I never wanted to go to college, my goal was to go to prison and survive. I knew when I got out I would gain more respect and my fellow gangsters would look at me like a hero because I withstood the lockup.

Unfortunately, prison is not a deterrent for most criminals, because while you are there you can learn all kinds of new techniques in the world of crime. It is like an advanced criminal college education system.

However, being incarcerated was no vacation; we did have to watch out for rival gangs inside the same facility who wanted to take you out. It is not easy to protect yourself inside prison. If someone is able to manufacture a weapon, you are certainly at a disadvantage. I was determined not to be a victim.

When you are locked away in a cell for twenty-three hours in a day, your mind devises all different kinds of ingenious ways to manufacture weapons. I made a shank out of one of the steel legs from my bed.

Each day I utilized the elastic in the waistband of my boxers and rubbed it on the steel to create friction and heat. Once the steel got hot I could bend it. It took days to finally get to the place where I could cut through the steel, but I had the time. What else was I going to do?

Once I had the piece of steel, I utilized the concrete floor and walls to help grind down one end of it into a sharp point. I had an effective bone-crusher; that is what we called them.

I have made weapons out of plastic Coke bottles, toothbrushes, and even newspapers. Often, we took a little piece of a razor blade and melted it into the handle of our toothbrush. We called these items little tomahawks or slicers. We used them to cut either the face or throat of a fellow prisoner. If you saw anyone cut on the face you knew they were rejected by their gang and it usually meant a death sentence. If someone was cut on the neck they often did not survive because they would bleed out.

I actually loved being in prison. For me it was the ultimate gladiator games. You knew any day you could get wacked or you could be the person carrying out a deadly plan of action. Talk about a debased sense of reality.

Inside the prison, it was always important to remain the big dog on top. You had to keep people afraid of you. It was most certainly the "Lord of the Files." My influence was felt throughout the facility, not even the guards were immune to it.

At this one facility, several gang members and I were trying to pressure a guard to work for us. We wanted him to smuggle drugs to us in the middle of the night. He was not buying into it. In fact, he became verbally abusive and told us we were nothing but worthless troublemakers who had no power over him. I was determined to make sure he knew differently.

One night, I managed to get word to some Mexican Mafia members on the outside to visit the guard at his home. When he arrived at his house, they were waiting on him. They beat him quite viciously. When he returned to work he was quite a different person. He did not join us, but he did not mess with us either.

At the time, I loved the power I had as a member of the Mexican Mafia. It did not matter the situation, the organization had people they could influence to get things done. Judges, politicians, lawyers, police officers, Drug Enforcement Agency and government personnel; it did not matter who they were, we had influence over them.

Being a part of that organization meant power, but it also brought danger that eventually soured me on the group. If someone higher up in the echelon of control decided they did not like you, your name went in the hat. This meant you were scheduled for extermination. It did not matter how loyal you were or how much you did for the organization, one guy in a bad mood could have you killed. There was no talking your way out of it. It was nothing but a game to them.

A group originally formed to protect their own morphed into one killing each other.

The Mexican Mafia gave me something I never received from home; love and acceptance. Looking back now, I know had my parents only loved me I could have been someone very different. I could have been a lawyer, a doctor, or maybe even a Marine. I had always been very driven about accomplishing my goals; unfortunately, I had the wrong people in charge of my life. If you hear nothing else from what I have shared please hear these words. Parents, love your children with all your heart for you hold their life within your hands.

After spending ten years in the California Prison System I was finally paroled. Life was going to have to change for me now that I was out. Through the conjugal visits with my girlfriend I had a baby girl for which I was responsible. We married shortly after I got out, so I knew my life as a gangster had to end. Somewhere deep down I knew I had lived a life of wickedness and I did not want my daughter or wife to feel its influence.

The problem was I really did not know how to do anything else. The only way I knew how to make money was selling drugs. I went back to my old neighborhood and bought a kilo of cocaine for about eighteen thousand dollars. I still had money stashed away from my old days of dealing so I used it to purchase the coke. I took the stash and cut it. It was so good I managed to turn my eighteen thousand dollar investment into one hundred thousand dollars in a very short amount of time. I was back in business.

I took that money and used it to buy a house, but I put the deed in the name of my in-laws. I did not want to risk my family losing our home should I end up back in prison. Over the next couple of years we had another daughter and then a son. Life seemed normal for me, well, as normal as it can be for someone who is secretly selling drugs behind the back of his family.

Cocaine was big business for me. It was the drug of choice for the rich. Lawyers, politicians, rock stars, celebrities; it did not matter to the clientele, it was their designer fix. They viewed it as the cool thing to do at their parties and I was happy to be their supplier.

Every Saturday brought the same routine. I would get up and travel across town to where I had another apartment. It was the place where I kept all my drugs and stashes of money, my base of operations you might say. I knew what I was doing was wrong, but the love of being a gangster had me hooked. The power I held over people was incredible. I could walk into a nightclub and immediately several complimentary drinks would be placed on the bar. They knew who I was and the control I wielded in the neighborhood.

I was determined to rule this game. I read everything I could get my hands on about the major mob and crime families around the world. I loved the stories of the Gambino and Lucchese crime families from New York. I tried to learn everything I could to be a successful gangster.

I did my best to keep everything as secretive as possible. I was working at a car dealership during the week and selling drugs on the weekend. I was determined to be successful in everything I did and one goal I wanted to attain was to get my high school diploma. To achieve that, I knew I had to attend night school.

Every evening I went to class and learned everything I could. Even though it was several years since I was in school, I ran into other people I knew back in the day who were also there trying to get their diploma. For the most part it was no big deal until I saw one of my enemies from high school. Armando was a guy I hated. He was a member of a rival gang back then and as soon as I saw him I knew I wanted him dead. The next night would be his last.

When Wednesday arrived, I went to class as usual, just waiting for it to end. I had more important things to do tonight. As soon as class was over, I stepped outside and waited for Armando. When he stepped out of his classroom I said to myself, "There is that punk, I am going to stab him." There was no hesitation, no second thoughts, my mind was made up.

I made my way toward Armando with evil in my heart. When I got right in front of him I stopped and said, "What's up, you remember me punk? I got something for you." What occurred next totally blew my mind.

"Yeah Erik, I remember you. I want to tell you that Jesus loves you. He can totally change your life." I staggered back and said, "What?" I had no clue what was going on. He threw my whole game plan out the window. I did not understand what was happening. Here I am about to put holes in this guy's body and he is telling me about the Christ.

I tried to speak but no words were coming out. However, Armando had plenty to say. He told me everything about what God did for him. Before I knew it, he invited me to a Bible study.

Was this some kind of joke? Was someone trying to pull one over on me? Life had just thrown me a screwball and I was left standing at the plate wondering what happened.

As crazy as it sounds, I agreed to go with him. It felt weird for me to walk into a Bible study with my enemy. I did not go to church, let alone a study group about the Bible, but deep down I knew I was supposed to be there. I was in a daze, but the words were sinking in. I did not understand what was happening, but something grabbed ahold of me. It was a power I never before experienced. I left there confused, but since I knew I needed to learn more I agreed to go to church with him the next Sunday.

You should have seen the faces of the people when I walked into church. I think they thought the roof was going to fall in because I was in the building. The people in attendance knew who I was and my reputation. It felt awkward, but I knew I was destined to be there. God had just totally blown my mind.

At the end of the service, I walked the aisle and made a new commitment. My life did not belong to me anymore; it belonged to Jesus Christ. I was determined to let Him direct my life the way He saw fit. I was ready for a total transformation. I wanted to learn everything I could about God, Jesus, and the Bible. I was so thankful, tears ran down my face as I just thanked God for giving someone like me a second chance at life.

Imagine the surprise on my wife's face when I told her the news. She was speechless, but she gladly welcomed the change. Life became new to us all. I made sure every time the doors of the church were open I had my family in attendance. It was not long thereafter my wife placed her life into the hands of Christ. My children were so happy and excited. It took a long time to get there, but we were a family finally on the right path. The criminal activity all stopped and the next five years were truly an amazement.

Too bad it did not stay that way.

Throughout those five years I was constantly getting calls and invitations from my gangster buddies to come and join them for things. It was a struggle at times, but I managed to steer clear from those pitfalls until a terrible event rocked my world.

My sister-in-law was having some serious relationship troubles with her husband, so she called my wife and asked her to come over for the evening. I was very supportive and told her she should go. I said, "I will watch the kids, you go and see what you can do to help." As the evening hours ticked away I knew something was wrong because she did not come home. In fact, she was gone for fifteen days. I had no clue where she was or what was going on. I questioned my sister-in-law, but I was getting no answers. Something was definitely up.

When she walked in the door after being gone for more than two weeks, the truth of her whereabouts were finally answered. She had been with another man. I was disgusted, devastated and sick. I could not believe what she did and I knew then my life with her was over.

After things fell apart in my marriage and we divorced, I just flat out rebelled. I really was down hearted and distraught. I felt I had been betrayed by God, even though I now know differently, at the time it felt that way to me. I returned to the lifestyle I knew the best; the life of a drug dealing gangster.

When you go back to the streets after living a good life, things just seem to spiral out of control quickly. I most certainly had an attitude and was not about to take any smack from anyone, especially any punk who crossed me in the hood.

One night while walking the streets of Richmond, California, I was approached by one of my enemies. I had already whipped him years before, but I guess he felt he could take me. So, when he came right out and said he wanted to fight I was more than willing to thrash him. It did not take long for me to leave him busted up on the sidewalk. Within moments he stumbled to his feet and said he would be back with reinforcements. He yelled, "When my brother gets out of prison you are going to pay big time." With a look of sheer consternation written all over my face I said, "Tell your brother, tell your mother, tell your dad, it don't matter, I will beat all of you."

A few weeks passed and sure enough here came his brother up to me on the street. I guess since he had just been released from prison he thought he was a bad dude. He came right into my face and said, "What's up?" I stood firm and said, "What's up?" He then tried to play coy by asking me where I was from. I told him he knew where I was from, now shut up and fight.

Fists flew left and right as a huge brawl began. He ended up just like his brother, on the sidewalk bleeding. Neither one of them were a match for me. I was feeling like the king of the streets once again.

On Thanksgiving, which was about two weeks after the fight, I was stopped at a gas station in the middle of the day putting fuel in my car. From out of nowhere I began to hear something hitting my car. Before I could turn all the way around I realized the guys I beat were shooting at me. I tried to get down and use my door as a shield, but it was too late. I felt the heat of two bullets enter my stomach. The warmth of the blood began to ooze down the front of my body and onto my legs.

My body crashed to the ground as I crawled across the asphalt trying to get into my car. I did not know how bad I was, but instinctively I knew I had to fight back. Once I got to the door of my car I pulled my body up into the seat and reached into my glove department where I pulled out my .45 caliber pistol. Without a moment to spare I fired shot after shot into their direction making direct contact with their car. Holes began to appear everywhere down the side of their vehicle. I was doing serious damage so they decided they better hightail it out of there.

I was glad they left, but I knew I was in trouble in more ways than one. I knew if I stayed there I would eventually bleed out. However, if I called for help the police would find my gun and I did not want that to happen either. I did not want to risk anything that could possibly be misconstrued and send me back to prison. So I did the only thing I could, I drove home. It was not easy to drive and attempt to keep yourself alive at the same time.

Once I arrived, I managed to get into the house where I left my gun. I then went back to the car. I figured I could not stay there because I did need medical help so I drove back to the scene of the shooting and called 911 from there. It was a foolish thing to do because I almost died, but I knew I could not risk going back to prison.

When the ambulance arrived they could not believe I was the only person who had been shot because there was so much blood all over. They immediately got me into the ambulance and took me to the emergency room.

When the physician came in to see me, he asked what happened. I simply replied, "I got shot, someone must have confused me with someone else." I was not fooling anyone, he could tell by the tattoos all over my body that what happened to me was gang related. Nevertheless, he went about putting me back together.

I was in the hospital for about two days before I was released. One of the first things I did once I got out was to call my kids. When my oldest daughter answered the phone she immediately began to ask me, "Daddy, we have not heard from you for two whole days, what is going on, what happened?" I called my kids every day twice a day back then, so when they did not hear from me a red flag went up immediately.

I told her nothing happened, everything was okay, but she was not buying it. She kept pressuring me until I finally told her I was shot. It really hit home to me at that moment. My drug dealing gangster lifestyle was going to take me away from my children forever if something did not change.

An intense struggle was happening inside me. The old Erik was doing battle with the new Erik. Part of me loved the gangster lifestyle, but the other part of me wanted to serve God again. There was a desire and hunger to walk close with the Lord. I was absolutely miserable and felt like the story of the son who was slopping hogs instead of living a life of fulfilment at home with his father. I was the ultimate prodigal son. It was time to come home, so I dropped to my knees and fell into the loving arms of my Heavenly Father who graciously forgave me once again.

My life has changed dramatically since those days long ago on the street. I have a new wife, a successful business, and the best kids in the world. I have learned things the hard way and I never want my children to experience the things I did when I was young. Life is still a struggle at times, but I am not leaning on my own strength, I am now relying on Christ and Him alone.

I still go back to the old neighborhood from time to time, but now I go with a new mission. I don't go to fight. I go to introduce them to the One who changed my life. I tell them they don't have to die, but they can live by embracing the One who died to make them new. It is an amazing sight to see guys who once were my enemies now standing beside me praising the Lord. He is truly the answer for the troubles in our society.

Before I sign off I want to leave to my children this message. Get ahold of yourself and think before you react. When you don't play by the rules you will get dealt a losing hand. At the end of the day always remember this; God is good. If it were not for the love of Christ I would still be in bondage, but today because of His sacrifice I will forever live in the land of the free.

And the Home of the Brave

Icould feel the movement of my every heartbeat. Adrenalin was coursing through my veins at breakneck speed. I looked out the door and saw the deep blue ocean far below us. The ships dotting the watery landscape created an intimidating picture. The seconds ticked away one by one until time ran out. It was now the appointed hour to make our move. I steadied my nerves as I raced toward the open door. Within a split second I hurled my body out of the plane and into the vast darkness of the early morning sky. D-Day had finally arrived. My name is Jake and this is my story.

A lot has changed since the day I entered the world in 1923. I was born on a small farm in Ohio just north of Columbus in a little place called Johnstown. You can probably only imagine what it was like for a family of eight, mom, dad and six kids, growing up during the time of the Great Depression. It was hard, but we stuck together and managed to get by.

School was pretty much just school to me, but I did participate in a lot of different activities. While in high school, I played on our football team where I made All-State as a halfback. Even though I was not very big, I was amazingly fast. I attribute a lot of that to the fact I ran from the school to my home each day. That was anywhere from two and a half to three miles one way depending on the route I took.

My talents on the athletic field attracted the attention of Capital University and they offered me a scholarship to play football at their school. However, in those days, the scholarships only covered two hundred and fifty dollars. Since my father worked for a dollar a day, the reality of me attending the university was not likely to happen. I decided when I graduated I would join the military instead.

That decision became even more emboldened in my spirit after December 7th, 1941. The attack on Pearl Harbor was not only personal to me; it was a direct slap in the face of every red-blooded American boy in my school. It was unbelievable to us something like that was happening to our country. In fact, almost every one of us who graduated that year joined a branch of the military. We were not about to sit back and let someone attack America without putting up a fight.

Many guys were drafted into the service, but I voluntarily enlisted in the Army Airborne on November the 28th of 1942. At that time you couldn't be married or wear glasses. You had to be in perfect health to even be considered. Out of 2400 recruits, the Army got 130 paratroopers. The training was so difficult, few made it through to the end.

There was an honor about that group of guys. We were not about to let people come into our country and kill our family and friends. To this day, any time I go to Pearl Harbor and view the Arizona Memorial, beads of sweat cover my brow. Far too often people who view the memorial do not respect the men who died there. It makes me furious to see them joking, laughing, and showing disrespect.

I wanted to join the paratroopers for two specific reasons. The first reason is obvious, I wanted to serve my country and protect my homeland. The second reason was, not only did I get the basic pay of fifty dollars a month from the Army, I also got one hundred dollars a month for being a paratrooper. Like I said before, my dad worked for one dollar a day, so that was an awful lot of money to me. I ended up sending most of my pay home to my family. I figured they could use it more than I could. I had food, clothing, and shelter with the Army. Some guys just blew their money, but I felt like sending it home was the right thing to do.

When I first joined the service I enlisted at Fort Hayes which was outside of Columbus Ohio. I was shipped from there to Camp Toccoa near Fort Benning, Georgia. We were one of the first airborne outfits located there. I became a member of the 508 Parachute Infantry Regiment which was part of the 82nd Airborne, the granddaddy of all airborne divisions.

I did my basic training at Camp Blanding in Florida. It was there I learned all the basics of shooting weapons, handling mortars, and the rigors of being a soldier.

During my entire time at the base I never went on a weekend pass. I always sent my money home. Imagine my surprise when I came down with the German measles. I have no clue how I contracted the virus. I had not been out of the camp and no one else in my company was sick.

I was hospitalized for a couple of days when one of the guys from my company poked his head in my room and said, "Hey Jake, we are moving out today." I sat up in the bed and said, "What do you mean you are moving out today?" I was so confused. I had no clue what was going on.

"Yeah, we are going to Fort Benning, we are going to do our jump training." As soon as I heard him speak those words, I was immediately up out of the bed and down at the nurse's station. I told her I had to get out of there. She disagreed and explained in no uncertain terms that I would not be leaving the hospital.

I guess she didn't realized how determined I was. It didn't matter to me I was only wearing the nightshirt they provided. I had my mind settled. I was leaving that day. I was not going to be left behind. When I got back to my room I climbed out the window and immediately ran down the street to the barracks.

When I arrived, the sergeant asked me, "What are you doing here?" I boldly said, "You guys are not moving out and leaving me here. I am going with you and no one is going to stop me." I guess he liked my determination because he did not say another word. He just motioned for me to get my gear and suit up.

Had the guy from my company not stopped by to tell me they were leaving I would have never known. I would have never ended up with that group of guys. I believe it was one of those instances of Divine guidance in my life. It most certainly would not be the last.

My training at Fort Benning began with me learning to pack my own parachute. By this time I was nineteen-years-old and still wet behind the ears. The next phase would be to jump. I can tell you the first time you make a jump you just pray you have packed your chute correctly.

Actually, my first jump was really not that bad. It was the fifth jump that had me the most concerned. It took five jumps for you to become a qualified paratrooper. The first four were easy for me, but I almost did not go on the last one. It was a lot of pressure because you knew once it was over you would get your jump boots, your wings, and a furlough home. I guess it was the anticipation or the nervousness about what came next that had me uneasy about the jump.

Regardless of the situation I knew I had to make the leap, so when they yelled, "Stand up and hook up," I did what was commanded. I figured if the rest of the guys could do it, then so could I. Needless to say, I successfully made the jump. I was a full-fledged paratrooper.

Most of the guys took advantage of their furlough and immediately headed home. That was not the case for me. Instead of returning to Ohio, I decided to stay around and attend demolition school where I learned to work with high explosives. I figured since I would be heading to war I might need to know about those things. I also took compass school, airplane identification training, and anything else I could learn. I was determined to be well educated.

With my training complete I headed home for a short visit before heading to Camp McCall in North Carolina. It was there I learned how to fight in the swamps. They were preparing us to fight the enemy who attacked our Naval Base at Pearl Harbor.

I enjoyed being in the paratroopers even though from the very beginning the Army tried to talk me out of it. They told each one of us when we entered combat to be prepared to experience an eighty-five percent casualty rate. That can be anything from killed in action, missing in action, wounded or captured. They told us that before we ever made our first jump and yet I was undeterred. I knew it was what I was destined to do.

With our training complete, it was time for us to move out, so in December of 1943 they transported us to Camp Shanks in New York. However, the plans for us had changed. We were headed to Europe instead of the Pacific.

It was just before Christmas on December 23rd when we boarded the USS James Parker and took off for Europe. Normally this would not have been any big deal, but the German Wolfpack had submarines in the Atlantic sinking our ships. Even off the coast of Florida, about three to five miles out they were torpedoing our sailing vessels. Many people do not realize how close the Germans were to landing on American soil.

When we started our voyage, we had the largest convoy going at that time. The USS James Parker was the flagship. We zigzagged across the ocean to avoid detection and it took us eleven days before we arrived in Belfast, Ireland.

The ship I was on carried over four thousand paratroopers. Unfortunately, we did lose a couple of ships crossing the Atlantic. Thousands of lives were lost because of those German torpedoes. We did however manage to destroy five or six of their submarines in the process of our crossing.

Making the journey was not an easy one. I was ten decks below near the bottom of the vessel and after that first night I slept on deck the rest of the trip. I figured if we got hit by a torpedo I would have no chance at survival if I was that far down in the ship. In fact, four of us slept right between the smoke stacks. The only time we went below deck was to get some chow and then we headed straight back on top.

Our unit was a specialty group. We had very valuable specific training for the Allied command. It is hard for me to say this, but we were trained to kill. I grew up just a small town farm boy, but the Army taught me how to take a man's life with exacting precision.

When we arrived in Belfast we did not stay there for long. There was not much daylight during that time of the year so we did not have the ability to train properly. From there we were routed to Nottingham, England where we trained right in the middle of Sherwood Forest starting in January of 1944.

I knew at some point we would be transported into the middle of the battle, but we had no clue when we would go. Our training took on more and more specifics. We did packing and re-packing of our field bundles, practice jumps, and field exercises. Everything was geared toward preparing us for the greatest test we would ever face.

We studied sandboxes that laid out the location around where we would be landing. We learned to recognize churches, bridges, and railroad tracks. We studied any identifying landmarks so we would be ready once we hit the ground.

Somewhere around the latter part of May they took all of us who were going to be a part of the mission and fenced us together on Folkingham Air Base. Nobody was allowed in and nobody was allowed out, only the supply people had access. There was security everywhere. We were under strict watch.

Every effort was made to keep all of us at ease, but it was not a complete success. There were accidents happening all around from the anxiousness of the men. Grenades were thrown out of the hanger because of a soldier accidentally pulling the pin, and that was just one of several issues we had.

One poor guy put a hole in the roof of the hanger when he mistakenly pulled the trigger on his M-1 while he was cleaning it. At least no one was wounded in that mishap unlike the poor paratrooper who was shot in the mouth by a pistol misfiring.

Thankfully, the time to leave was close at hand. We were briefed on the exact location of where we were going, the actual day of the planned attack and what we were to do once we hit the ground. We would parachute several miles in from the coast and our orders were to take no prisoners for the first ten days. While on the ground we were to set up road blocks and do anything necessary to keep the enemy from getting to those beaches.

We knew what we were up against. We were aware of how the Germans executed about half of the 600 people of the Village of Limoges France. If that were not bad enough, they barricaded the other 300 into a small church and set it on fire. Women and children perished mercilessly amongst the flames. Anyone trying to escape was shot down in cold blood. That was our adversary.

As the day of operation drew closer, our anxiety levels reached an all-time high. Many were ready, some were nervous, and all of us had a sense of fear tempered with the obligation this had to be done. The fate of the entire planet rested in us stopping this fascist war machine.

On the night of June 4th, our original day to deploy, we were rained out, so it was back to the waiting game. The weather was so bad we had no choice, we could not go. All day long on the 5th we waited, wondering what would happen and then the phone rang. It was on; we were heading to Normandy. We were to parachute into France first thing on June 6th; D-Day had finally arrived.

Soldiers, Sailors and Airmen of the Allied Expeditionary Force!

You are about to embark upon the Great Crusade, toward which we have striven these many months. The eyes of the world are upon you. The hopes and prayers of liberty-loving people everywhere march with you. In company with our brave Allies and brothers-in-arms on other Fronts you will bring about the destruction of the German war machine, the elimination of Nazi tyranny over oppressed peoples of Europe, and security for ourselves in a free world.

Your task will not be an easy one. Your enemy is well trained, well equipped and battle-hardened. He will fight savagely.

But this is the year 1944. Much has happened since the Nazi triumphs of 1940–41. The United Nations have inflicted upon the Germans great defeats, in open battle, man-to-man. Our air offensive has seriously reduced their strength in the air and their capacity to wage war on the ground. Our Home Fronts have given us an overwhelming superiority in weapons and munitions of war, and placed at our disposal great reserves of trained fighting men. The tide has turned. The free men of the world are marching together to victory.

I have full confidence in your courage, devotion to duty, and skill in battle. We will accept nothing less than full Victory!

Good Luck! And let us all beseech the blessing of Almighty God upon this great and noble undertaking.

—Dwight D. Eisenhower

I got my gear together. It was time to load the planes. The months, weeks, and days of training were complete. My next jump would not be a practice run; it would be the real thing.

That entire evening I spent eating donuts and drinking coffee. I figured it would be quite some time before I would get to enjoy those items again. I don't know what it is about being a farm kid, but I was always hungry.

When the plane rumbled down the runway, my mind pondered the war. We were not in the air very long when my thoughts began to change to my stomach. All those donuts were having a bad effect on me. For the first time I began to feel air sick. I would just have to ignore it, there was nothing else I could do.

As the plane flew along, I remember the night was clear. There were very few clouds in the sky. I kept thinking, "What am I doing here? What am I going to encounter when I hit the ground? Can I really kill someone?" I didn't know if I would ever again see the peaceful little village in Ohio I fondly called home.

Just as we flew over the Jersey and Guernsey Islands, anti-aircraft fire began to light up the sky. The Germans controlled those islands and they hit a few of our planes. I wondered if I would even get the chance to jump.

I stood up and moved over to the door. The churning of my stomach was in full motion. As we flew along headed to our drop point I was feeling really sick. I tried to keep it down but it was no use, the coffee and donuts decided they needed to see the light of day. Needless to say the guys were not happy with me because I caused many others to vomit as well.

No sooner had I went back to my seat and sat down I heard the orders, "Stand up and hook up." The commands came loud and clear through the hull of the plane. It was no easy task to stand. We weighed over three hundred pounds with all our gear.

The familiar sound-off for equipment check rang throughout the hull of the aircraft, "16, OK, 14, OK," and right down through the group. The time had finally arrived to jump. My rifle was tucked beneath my vest close to my chest. We had to strap the weapon against us so it would not get dislodged or caught in our chute. In my heart I knew if the Germans saw us coming we would be sitting ducks just waiting to be shot out of the sky.

The green light came on signaling it was time to go. When I leaped into the darkness, just after 1:00 a.m. on June 6th, 1944, I felt the jolt of my parachute as it opened. I floated through the night sky headed for parts unknown. I could see fires burning in the distance as the ground came closer into view.

I grabbed the risers of my chute and began to steer my way to safety. Unfortunately I missed the ground and landed in a tree located inside a small church yard. This was not the best place to land for many reasons. For one, I could have really been hurt by the branches, some guys died having been punctured by a limb. Also, if I got stuck, the enemy would have a clear advantage over me.

Thankfully for me the tree was only about twenty feet high. I was hanging about eight to ten feet above the ground and I was totally scared to death. I had no clue where the enemy was and what I was going to do once I got down.

A young French girl about fourteen-years-old, watched out the window as the paratroopers descended upon her town. She was so hopeful the brave men coming from the sky would liberate her country from the clutches of evil. All around her home and in her yard were German soldiers camped out for the night. She actually saw me land in the tree some forty yards from her home. I later learned she prayed I would not be found. Her prayers were most certainly answered.

Amazingly, I was not detected by the enemy, so I was able to take my knife out of its case and cut through the straps of my parachute so I could get on the ground. Originally, I didn't want to land in that tree, but in all actuality it saved my life. It would not be the first time the grace of God shined miraculously on this farm boy from Ohio.

After I was cut free, I made a beeline for the hedgerow. I wanted to make sure I was not seen. The area where I landed was incredibly dark and the sounds of the night closed in all around me. I stayed by that hedge for what seemed like hours before I finally realized I was all alone. I kept hearing gunfire from all directions. I knew I could not stay there so I decided I better try and find someone from my unit.

I slowly made my way down the hedgerow. I crossed a small dirt lane where I continued to creep along carefully for about a mile. When I got to the end of the lane there was a small stone wall. I cautiously moved through an opening when I heard the sound of approaching footsteps. I knew it could not be our guys because the formation was too large. It had to be the Germans.

I decided I was not going to take any chances, so I immediately jumped over the wall and slid down the hill where I landed in a nice fresh batch of cow manure or a cow pile as we called it on the farm. It was all over my boots and half way up my pants leg. There was nothing I could do but stay in it and be quiet.

As I laid there in disgust, half gagging from the smell, I could hear German voices as a platoon sized group of soldiers passed by. They were close, but they did not see me. I was grateful once they were out of range. I got up and tried to clean myself off but it was to no avail. I ended up having to wear that manure covered uniform for the next thirty-seven days. Never once did I have the opportunity to take a bath or eat a hot meal. It was not something I would wish on anyone, but you might say I truly blended in with my surroundings.

As the night slowly crept along I knew one thing for sure, I found the Germans, but I had not found my unit and that would have to be my primary objective. As I cautiously stood, a large sound came swooping in above my head. A British Horsa, which is a troop carrying glider, passed directly above me and crashed as it hit the ground near the hedgerow.

I wasn't sure what to do at first but I decided I had to see if there were any survivors. When I arrived on the scene it was not good. Dead bodies were everywhere, but several men survived. I hung around for a few moments and talked to the survivors, but there was really nothing I could do because I was not a medic. I knew I had to find my outfit and I had to find them soon.

I headed back up to the hedgerow and decided to hide out until daylight. I dug myself a slit trench and crawled inside. I managed to sleep a little off and on until morning arrived. At the crack of dawn, I slowly moved from the trench and crawled toward a farm house in the distance. As I neared the farmyard, I could see Germans. I decided I could not risk being caught, so I headed back to the hedgerow.

For the next four days I played hide and seek with those guys. I knew if I was to get caught it would jeopardize my mission so I did my best to stay out of their sight. That continued until the sixth day when I finally spotted some troopers from the 101st.

Those guys were twenty miles from their drop zone. Normally, the paratroop planes flew in a formation, but because of the anti-air-craft fire we encountered, we all became separated. Men who were supposed to be together ended up all over the countryside. These troopers were not from my unit, but it did not matter, I was just glad they were Americans.

Over the course of the next several days I stayed on patrol with this unit while trying to find H Company of the 508 Parachute Infantry Regiment. That was my outfit and I had to find them.

Finally, on the tenth day we came into a small village and there was the 82nd Airborne unit. I finally found my squad, my platoon, my company. Of course a buddy of mine had to give me flak and say, "Hey Jake where have you been? Goofing off I guess." I just laughed and told him, "Oh, here and there. I have been all over trying to find you guys. What have you been doing hiding out from the war?" We both smiled. He was glad to see me and I was glad to see him.

A few days after I was reunited with my unit, we left the village and crossed over the Merderet River. Unbeknownst to us, the Germans were waiting on the other side. Immediately, shots were fired at us. We managed to gain some ground as we fought through the orchard. The firing of artillery was so deadly guys on both sides were dropping fast.

We crossed over a couple of small roads until we came to a stone wall. The Germans were firing from behind it. By this time I had my machine gun fully deployed and was shooting at every enemy target I could find. I was stationed down in a foxhole left behind from the German soldiers so I had good cover.

Moments later, a couple of 88-mm shells landed all around my foxhole filling it with dirt and debris, but I was unscathed by the explosion. As I left my place of cover with my folding stock rifle I made my way toward the small wall. Everything was extremely quiet, too quiet for my comfort.

As I surveyed the open field, a man appeared out of the corner of my eye. He was only about fifty yards in front of me As I turned my weapon to fire I realized it was a German medic. He walked slowly over to one of his men lying on the ground. He picked up the wounded German soldier and placed him on the back of his shoulders. When he turned to leave, I noticed a red cross on his back so I lowered my weapon and did not shoot. I yelled to our guys to hold their fire. The medic climbed over the stone wall then moments later disappeared out of sight.

I figured this was the last I would see of him, but it was not. About fifteen minutes later, he returned with sixty-one German soldiers. Yet, they had not come to fight, they came to surrender. I realized had we shot that medic we would have never caught those German soldiers.

The soldiers were not all from Germany, most of them had been pressed into the service of the Nazis after their homeland was overthrown. In fact, they seemed quite grateful we were there.

Now remember, we were told we were to take no prisoners. We were to kill every German soldier we encountered. I pondered to myself if we were about to shoot these sixty-one guys. We decided against it. We located a large barn and locked them inside placing a guard at each end. When the command behind us arrived we turned the prisoners over to them. I do not know what happened to those guys, I just knew it did not seem right to shoot someone who had voluntarily surrendered.

★ ★ ★

Being a paratrooper meant you were usually surrounded. You fought a battle of some sort every day, but I had yet to experience the kind of fight that was waiting for me on July 4th, 1944.

The morning started with a slight fog. Mist settled on the ground overnight. It always felt cold in the early hours, but on this day the weather seemed to be much colder. I was called upon to lead an offensive against a fortified hillside. I had recently been promoted due to the fact we lost so many men. The commanding officers gave us instructions to move forward. Our mission was to take the area and hillside in front of us.

H Company, which was my unit, led the frontal attack as we moved into the field. There were twenty-four in my group. On top of the hill in prime position was a Hitler Youth Division. These young soldiers were fanatics. They were effectively brain-washed with Nazi propaganda most of their lives. They immediately began to rain down mortar and machine gun fire all around us. If that were not bad enough, we soon realized we were in a German mine field.

Explosions, followed by screams and cries of "I'm hit," cascaded all around me. My men were dropping fast, so I gave the orders to head to the right, straight down the field away from the hill. I felt a bullet pierce through the collar of my jump jacket, but it touched none of me. I have no clue how it missed but I did not care, I just kept running. I was so frustrated at the slowness of my feet; it was as if they were running in quick sand.

With every step I took I was praying to God. I really did not believe I was going to get out alive. I was not only afraid, I was terrified, but I had to make sure my men got to safety. When we managed to reach the hedgerow at the end of the field we finally had some cover. As I peered out into the open I could see my friends, Bryant, Ray, and Dick lying in a crumpled heap. Their bodies had been torn apart by the machine gun fire. I felt sick, angry, and devastated all at the same time. War was most certainly Hell.

Finally, I saw the exact place from where the machine gun was firing. I raised my M-1 rifle and took aim at the location. I had one bullet in the chamber and eight in the clip. With exacting precision I emptied my M-1 into where the machine gun nest was positioned.

Moments later it got deathly quiet. There were no birds chirping and no guns firing, only some rustling in the trees overhead. The shots from my M-1 were effective.

During the battle, most of us had become separated. Our instructions were to fall back to our main unit in case this happened. I looked to my right and saw a steep bank about twenty feet high. It was not the best option, but I had to go that way if I were to make it back to my outfit. Fear had a death grip on my legs, they did not want to move, but I knew I must climb that hill if I wanted to survive. The thought of trying to scale a hillside in the open had me terrified. I would be a sitting duck if there were still Germans nearby.

A cold sweat covered my body as I made my way from behind the hedgerow. Within seconds I was dashing across the field headed toward the bank. As I hit the bottom I scrambled up the side of the hill at breakneck speed. I reached the top and slid down the other side. I have no clue how I managed to get over it so fast or why I was not shot.

Then I was safe. I moved along for about fifty yards when I encountered another paratrooper sitting with his back against the wall. He was wounded. He motioned for me to get down. I lowered my body as close to the ground as I could while I moved in beside him. The bullet had struck him pretty hard and he could not walk. I waited a few minutes then told him I would get him back to safety. He told me I should go on without him. He complained of so much pain.

I was more determined than ever to put him over my shoulder and carry him, but he adamantly refused. He insisted he stay behind, so I opened my sulfur powder and put as much as I could on his wounds. Then I looked him in the eye promising to send back a medic.

It would be the last time I ever saw him. To this day it truly haunts me I had to leave him behind. I have often wondered if he ever made it out. I did eventually escape and notified the medics about him, but I never knew if he lived or died.

July 4th was a low point of all the battle action I saw during the Normandy Campaign. I fought every battle all the way to the end when we finally left on July 13th from Utah beach. H Company had 130 guys who went in, only thirty-nine of us returned. I was the only guy in my tent who survived.

After what I went through I had a new sense of appreciation for the last words of our Declaration of Independence. *"We mutually pledge to each other our Lives, our Fortunes and our sacred Honor."*

I got a much needed break after my time at Normandy. It wasn't very long, but a five day leave felt like a summer vacation after the battles I had just been through. When it was time to report back I knew I would have to prepare for our next mission. Hitler and the National Socialists had to be defeated. We all knew it would be difficult, but we were determined to win.

On September 17th of 1944, after a period of training, we boarded the planes bound for Holland. Operation Market Garden would be our next assignment. It would prove to be the largest airborne invasion in the history of the world at the time. The trip from England to Holland would be a short one by air. We were going to be dropped in about 100 miles behind enemy lines.

It was such a different trip then when we flew into Normandy for the D-Day invasion. On this mission we could actually see people down below waving their arms and flags for us. They were so hopeful we could defeat the Nazi war machine. After nearly four and a half years of oppression they saw us as liberators coming from the sky.

I remember getting up and walking over to the open door and looking at the countryside below. These were innocent people whose lives were stolen from them by the wicked tyrannical dictates of a mad man and his willing socialist accomplices.

Everything was going smoothly until we heard the loud booming sound of artillery and our plane was rocked by enemy fire. Smoke began to pour from the right engine as we all realized we were hit. Bodies began to leap from their seats as they made their way to the open door. If we wanted to survive we would have to exit immediately. There would be no waiting for us to reach our designated jump zone.

Without a moment to spare I soared out of the open door past the flames of the burning plane into the bomb filled sky. We were like clay pigeons at a skeet shoot. We had no way to defend ourselves as we descended from the heavens. Large black trails of billowing smoke left a streak across the firmament as the plane plunged to the ground making a huge hole as it exploded upon impact.

A couple of the other troopers and I managed to land unscathed in a nearby field, but we were far from safe. We were in the middle of enemy territory and they knew we were there.

As a paratrooper, you knew when you hit the ground you would have to begin fighting immediately. Within seconds upon landing, I was in a battle. Shots were being fired all around me. I had to get my weapon deployed and find cover. The entire unit was grasping for any place we could find where we would have a chance to regroup and charge the Nazis.

The combat would be bloody and difficult. We engaged the enemy for the next three days straight. Little food and sleep were the norms. I truly do not know how any of us survived, but we did.

On the 21st of September we came across a small house in the corner of an open field. I could tell the building had seen better days. It was still intact, but it had experienced its fair share of action. As we approached the structure we proceeded with caution. We could never be too careful in situations like these. We were fearful we might jump a group of German soldiers who were using the house for a base camp.

The door creaked slowly as we looked inside. At first we saw nothing, but then we heard movement up in the attic. Someone was definitely up there. With our weapons drawn we moved toward the area where we could access the attic. The moment was at hand. Would they get us or would we get them? With a loud crash we flung open the door revealing a young Jewish family huddled before us.

When they saw we were Americans, they were so relieved. One of the young girls cried out, "Please save our souls, the Nazis they are coming!" She was absolutely correct. Outside a German tank rumbled across the field toward the structure. Immediately, we fell into action. Rifles blazed with the flames of gun fire. One of my troops steadied his bazooka as the tank came within range. The sky echoed with a thunder-like sound as he fired his weapon. The shot screamed across the field finding its target with exacting precision. The tank took a direct hit in the side knocking it out of commission.

Shots were firing all around us, but we were determined to win this battle. Not only did our lives depend on it, but to this young family we were their liberators. The action lasted for a short time before the Germans were defeated.

After the battle, I found out the family of five had been hiding inside the attic of this home for twenty five months straight. They never left the structure the entire time for fear they would be caught and sent to a concentration camp. It may have not been the biggest battle of the war, but on this day it was certainly the most satisfying.

The next day we moved toward Berg en Dal. When we arrived, we began work digging our slit trenches for protection. I will never forget the kindness of a dear Dutch family in the area. A man and woman approached me explaining they had some hot food ready. They wanted our unit to come and eat. I willingly accepted their gracious offer and sent the men in two by two. The food was not extravagant, just fried potatoes, and some pieces of meat, but to me it was a meal fit for a king.

Once we were finished, I thanked the family and we moved on, but something began to bother me. I felt bad because I figured we had probably eaten all their food. However, later when we attacked the Groot Hotel we found a German division headquarters stationed in the facility. In the cellar of the hotel we discovered a massive hoard of food. We took those items back to the family who fed us and also delivered food to the people in the Village. It was such a gratifying experience.

Later on in the day, we were assembled near our slit trenches, we heard the distant rumble of German artillery. Then out of nowhere a shot exploded in our camp. Every one of us raced for cover. My buddy John dove into my trench and I landed directly on top of him just as a shell from a German Railroad Gun detonated beside us. The death rattle of the Nazi military machine found its mark.

The roar of the explosion was deafening. I felt the discharged shrapnel as it entered my leg, back, face and arms. The burning hot metal pierced my flesh like knives through butter. The helmet I was wearing had a hole in the middle of the back of it. Blood was everywhere and things looked pretty bad. I was writhing in pain, but I was still alive. John on the other hand was not. Even though he had been shielded from the attack by my body, he died in the explosion. I do not understand how I lived and he didn't. It was another one of those instances where the blessings of God clearly said, "It is not your time my friend."

Two of my men carried me back to the aid station where they began to address my wounds. I did not want to be there, asking to be taken back to my squad. I was informed they would need to do surgery on me immediately so I was sent to the division hospital instead.

I was transported to Nijmegen to one of the facilities formerly used as a Hitler baby factory. The Nazis had unwed mothers birthing babies for Hitler's elite SS troops, part of his master race plan. There were hundreds of baby buggies in the basement entry and throughout the hallways.

Regardless the location, they wasted no time in performing surgery to remove the shrapnel from my body. When I awoke, I noticed there were wounded soldiers everywhere. It was really a trying time. The doctor and nurse attending to me were very kind. I was transported outside the building into an area where they had tents erected for those who were recovering.

I was in the recovery area for no longer than about fifteen minutes when a German fighter plane flew overhead and began raining down terror from the sky. Their shells exploded into the makeshift hospital. The operating room where I had just been treated was destroyed. Sadly too were the doctor and nurse who saved my life.

We were moved the next day to another hospital before I was evacuated from Brussels and sent to a facility in Oxford, England before eventually settling in Coventry. Here is where I saw the true power of the German War Machine. They bombed the city so much, several parts of it were in shambles. Nonetheless, I spent the next three months there recovering from the wounds I received during the Market Garden operation.

I have heard many folks exclaim Market Garden was a failure. You just try and tell that to the family of Jews we rescued from Nazi tyranny if it was a failure or talk to the paratroopers who performed every one of their assigned tasks to the letter. I think you will get a more accurate account of the operation.

In December of 1944 after months of recovery time I was finally ready to return to the war. I was initially told I was going to be transferred to another unit. I was livid; there was no way I was going anywhere else. I came in with the 82nd Airborne, H Company, and I was determined I would leave with them.

Finally, after much persuasion, they agreed, so on December 15th I returned to my unit. Two days later we got word the Germans, via a surprise blitzkrieg, had thrust through Ardennes to Antwerp. I knew then we were headed to Belgium. The Battle of the Bulge would be my next theater of operation.

On the morning of the 18th at about 8:30 my unit and I were loaded onto large cattle trucks. They were semi-trailers with standing room only, with the sides about chest high to the men. We were so crowded, there was nowhere for us to sit, we had to stand the entire trip which took more than twenty hours. I was cold, hungry and miserable, but I knew I had a job to do. I had to be brave.

Short stops along the way allowed us to get off and seek some relief. It gave us the chance to prepare some hot coffee and eat our K-rations. The truck ride was not enjoyable at all. The men were mad as hell by the time we arrived. That did not bode well for the enemy.

During the trip, some of the 101st Airborne were forced to turn toward Bastogne while the 82nd continued to the Ardennes. To this day, if you ask a paratrooper about the battle, he will ignore the fierce fighting, short food rations, and lack of warm clothing to tell you all about that miserable truck ride.

When we finally reached our destination, fighting began before we could even leave the truck. H Company was constantly on the front lines of the battle. Every day brought much of the same things. Moving, fighting, digging fox holes, and braving the bitter cold with frost bitten feet, begging for rest, and hoping for hot food, but getting none; that was our existence. There were some days when it was twenty-three below zero. It was absolutely miserable.

The Germans wanted to get through Bastogne to Antwerp in order to release more than 100,000 garrisons of captured prisoners. Had they succeeded the war might have had a different outcome.

We fought through the entire month of December. We were forbidden from staying in a house because the Germans would shell the place if they saw us enter. By the time Christmas morning rolled around we were still in our defensive positions. Everyone was tired and hungry.

Starving and desiring some hot food, we decided to make our way down toward a small house. We weren't there very long before artillery began dropping. Immediately everyone headed outside for the foxholes. Unfortunately, I was the last man out of the building and was trapped inside when an 88 shell brought the roof down on my head.

My men began to call out, "Hey Sarge, are you alright?" I told them, "No, but I am alive so get me out of here!" They eventually dug me out and once again I survived another close call with death. What a Christmas that was, maybe those K rations would not be so bad to eat after all.

A few weeks later, we pulled back into a brush area with snow three feet deep and the temperature well below zero. Shots rang out from the distance as a sniper fired on our unit. Two of my men were killed by his deadly accuracy. I was so upset. I did not care anymore what happened to me. I figured I was not going to get out alive anyway, so my friend Charlie and I headed out to find that sniper.

Before we left Charlie looked at me and said, "We are not allowed to do this." I turned and bluntly said, "I am a staff sergeant and you are a private, so we are going!" That was the end of the conversation; Charlie fell in line behind me as we headed out through the snow.

With my M-1 in hand, I traveled about thirty or forty yards when I got a sixth sense something was wrong. I turned cautiously to my right where I saw the sniper lying on the ground about twenty feet directly in front of me.

A cold chill ran down my back. My time was up, he had me dead in his sights with his Mauser rifle pointing directly at my head. I should have been killed, but instead I slowly pointed my M-1 at him and yelled for him to throw down his weapons and put up his hands. To my surprise two Germans jumped up and did what I asked. They were both wearing snow capes and either one could have shot me. To this very day, I thank God for His Providence in the situation. It is the only explanation for why I am still alive.

Charlie came in behind me and we took the German soldiers into captivity. They seemed quite frightened and very young. We turned them over to our battalion and headed back to our unit. It was a difficult decision. These two men killed two of my guys. Everything inside of me screamed to just execute them for revenge, but I was an American, a paratrooper, and we could not do that. We had to do the honorable thing. It was the way I was trained and it was most certainly the way I was raised.

When evening arrived I spent most of the night digging a foxhole. I had become quite adept at this task. Not only did it provide a means of protection, the work to dig it also kept you from freezing to death. I found a little bit of hay in a nearby barn and lined the inside hoping to provide a somewhat comfortable night's sleep.

When morning arrived I had an awful feeling of dread. It was going to be a bad day. I had no way of explaining why I felt the way I did, but it was certainly evident to me. About that time, a runner came down and told me I was wanted up at the battalion command.

When I stood before the Commanding Officer he gave me instructions to take my squad down through a small path and knock out the 88 that had been shelling us. I told him, "Sir I only have six men." His response was to go anyway.

Not the words I wanted to hear, but I was determined to do my duty. I gathered my men and we headed toward the path. I was the lead as we walked down a small embankment leading through the forest. My squad all carried automatic weapons and I carried my M-1.

As we approached a curve in the road a deathly silence filled the air. Only the muffled sound of our footsteps could be heard. Then it happened, a sniper shot came out of nowhere and penetrated my chest. The bullet exited through my shoulder blade. I fell to the ground like I had been hit with a giant hammer.

I struggled to crawl next to a large tree when a second and third shot hit the bark above my head. I was in a desperate situation and losing large amounts of blood. That was the last thing I remember before I blacked out.

Sometime later, I was roused by an American medic who was taking my boots off. He was utterly shocked when I pulled my .45

pistol from my coat and said to him, "You might get my boots, but I promise you will never wear them. I am not dead just yet so put them back on." The young man began to weep. He had believed I was dead and paratrooper jump boots were prized possessions.

I was carried back to the aid station by two German prisoners we captured earlier in the day. There, I was temporarily treated, placed on a stretcher and taped from my neck to my waist. After I was prepared for transport they loaded me in the ambulance with several other guys and off we went to a division hospital in the Leige.

The night was intensely dark as we rumbled down the small road. I could feel every bump and hole as I bounced up and down on my stretcher directly behind the driver. The stretcher was nothing like a modern day unit; it was basically a long piece of fabric with two wooden poles on either side.

The journey was treacherous and before long things got interesting. The driver made a sharp turn as the ambulance hit a massive dip in the road. The momentum caused my stretcher to collapse. The thing folded up around me like I was wrapped in a burrito. I could not move. I was wedged in behind the driver seat and the other passengers.

I rode along in this condition for about a mile until we approached a large ridge. I could hear the sounds of artillery fire outside. It sounded like they were getting closer. Then it happened, one hit nearby. The explosion caused the driver to lose control as he swerved to avoid being hit. The ambulance went over the embankment and we rolled down the mountainside. Bodies flew around the inside of the vehicle all the while I was wedged tightly behind the seat of the driver.

When the ambulance finally came to a stop we were upside down in a shallow river bottom. I was really shook up, but I was still alive. I looked all around me and realized I was the only one who survived, yet there was nothing I could do. I was pinned inside the ambulance wedged in with no way out. It was just a little past midnight and I laid there thinking, *I wonder what is going to happen to me?* I began to pray and thank God for his mercy upon this small town farm boy from Ohio. I had no clue why I was the only one who was spared, but I was grateful I was still breathing.

When dawn finally arrived some American soldiers walking along the road at the top of the ridge spotted the ambulance below. Thankfully for me, they came down to investigate. I was never happier than when the door opened and those GIs looked in.

It took about thirty minutes to get me free and back up the side of the mountain. I was so thirsty, but a colonel in the group advised against giving me anything to drink because of the wound in my chest. As they loaded me onto the truck a soldier walking by said, "Hey, he's a paratrooper!" Somehow those words meant more than usual to me that day.

The Battle of the Bulge was the costliest action ever fought by our Army. More than 100,000 men were casualties. I was blessed to have been one of the few who survived.

Two hours later after being found in the ambulance, I was in the hospital in Leige where they operated on me. I woke up the next day at about 11:30 a.m. From there I was sent to Paris, then England, and finally I returned to America where I remained in Memphis General Hospital until August 25th, 1945. My time as a paratrooper was over.

★ ★ ★

It was a beautiful sunny day when I stepped off the Greyhound bus at the corner of two small streets in my hometown. There was nobody around as I walked slowly down the sidewalk and sat down on the bench. A Model-T Ford drove by, then a horse and buggy. I just sat there taking it all in before I began my 3½ mile walk to the farm where I grew up. My parents did not have a phone so there was no way to contact them.

When I finally arrived home, I stepped on the front porch and walked through the door. My mother and father immediately began to weep. A stack of telegrams stating I was wounded in action and missing in action were still lying on the table. They believed they probably would never see their son again. On more than forty occasions I should have been killed, but thanks to the blessings of God their boy returned.

I looked around the old farm house and realized just how good it was to be back home; Johnstown, Ohio, the home of the brave.

The Story of Liberty

It is March 1776 and the men in attendance are clearly focused on liberty. War has come to their homeland and the dictates of a tyrannical government have led them to this place. The imagination can only conceptualize the thoughts going through the mind of John Hancock, the president of the group known as the Continental Congress. If we could read his thoughts, I believe they would go something like the following passage.

The words I am about to write are serious, in fact they will be considered by some as treasonous. Yet, they must be written. I know of no other way to express the importance of this correspondence to my fellow countrymen.

We are facing calamity and distress. Our liberties have come under assault from an administration which is stealthily treacherous with a spirit inclined to revenge. We face fear, uncertainty, and a lack of direction. The question echoing from across the fruited plain is simply this, "What can be done?"

The answer is a simple one, and yet it comes so stubbornly to us for we are a proud people. We have turned savage wilderness into livable cities, desolate coasts into prosperous ports, and produced prosperity out of hardship. Yet now we are at the brink of losing it all to an overtaxing and burdensome government hell-bent on our submission. Where oh where shall we turn?

Dare I believe it to be true we have so lost our way? Have we forgotten from where our help comes? The people must know, they must be reminded how we can fight the battle and win. Stand up and listen fellow countrymen for the answer draws nigh.

Oh how we as a country have forgotten. We have traded morality for immorality, humility for arrogance, and faithfulness for dishonesty. The people will hear my words, they must hear my words. The very foundation and future depends on it. The enemy is waiting for us to fall. They taunt us with ridicule, belittle us with their pedigrees, and mock our beliefs, yet we shall not fail.

I pray for my country, for its citizens and for its safety. I know when they read these words they will be moved to action. They will remember who we are as a people. We will find "the Way, the Truth, and the Life" once again.

Wouldn't it be nice to know what those men we call our Founding Fathers were actually thinking in March of 1776. Unlike my thoughts above, we don't have to guess. We have their actual thoughts and desires written down on paper and faithfully secured in the United States Library of Congress. It is known as the National Day of Prayer Proclamation issued on March 16th of 1776. I believe if you read it carefully you will find out how America became the Land of Liberty.

In times of impending calamity and distress; when the liberties of America are imminently endangered by the secret machinations and open assaults of an insidious and vindictive administration, it becomes the indispensable duty of these hitherto free and happy colonies, with true penitence of heart, and the most reverent devotion, publicly to acknowledge the over ruling providence of God; to confess and deplore our offences against him; and to supplicate his interposition for

averting the threatened danger, and prospering our strenuous efforts in the cause of freedom, virtue, and posterity.

*The Congress, therefore, considering the warlike preparations of the British Ministry to subvert our invaluable rights and privileges, and to reduce us by fire and sword, by the savages of the wilderness, and our own domestics, to the most abject and ignominious bondage: are Desirous, at the same time, to have people of all ranks and degrees duly impressed with a solemn sense of God's superintending providence, and of their duty, devoutly to rely, in all their lawful enterprises, on his aid and direction, Do earnestly recommend, that Friday, the Seventeenth day of May next, be observed by the said colonies as a day of humiliation, fasting, and prayer; that we may, with united hearts, confess and bewail our manifold sins and transgressions, and, by a sincere repentance and amendment of life, appease his righteous displeasure, and, through the merits and mediation of **Jesus Christ**, obtain his pardon and forgiveness; humbly imploring his assistance to frustrate the cruel purposes of our unnatural enemies; and by inclining their hearts to justice and benevolence, prevent the further effusion of kindred blood.*

But if, continuing deaf to the voice of reason and humanity, and inflexibly bent, on desolation and war, they constrain us to repel their hostile invasions by open resistance, that it may please the Lord of Hosts, the God of Armies, to animate our officers and soldiers with invincible fortitude, to guard and protect them in the day of battle, and to crown the continental arms, by sea and land, with victory and success: Earnestly beseeching him to bless our civil rulers, and the representatives of the people, in their several assemblies and conventions; to preserve and strengthen their union, to inspire them with an ardent, disinterested love of their country; to give wisdom and stability to their counsels; and direct them to the most efficacious measures for establishing the rights of America on the most honorable and permanent basis - That he would be graciously pleased to bless all his people in these colonies with health and plenty, and grant that a spirit of

*incorruptible patriotism, and of pure undefiled religion, may univer-
sally prevail; and this continent be speedily restored to the blessings of
peace and liberty, and enabled to transmit them inviolate to the latest
posterity.*

*And it is recommended to Christians of all denominations, to
assemble for public worship, and abstain from servile labor on the
said day.*

Resolved, That the foregoing resolve be published.

March 16, 1776

Protect us by Thy might, Great God our King.

About the Author

D r. Michael T. George grew up in a small town in West Virginia, where the elements of faith, family and hard work were an everyday occurrence. Michael left home at the age of sixteen to pursue a private education in another part of his home state. It is here where Michael's desire to share the principles of life, liberty, faith, and freedom began to take full bloom.

A dynamic speaker with a gift for sharing inspirational messages has endeared him to people of all backgrounds. Realizing how the power of a story can change lives, lend hope and create a sense of unity, Michael travels the country artfully crafting stories of inspiration with a dramatic flare. His presentations weave together the principles of education and enlightenment.

Michael is the host of a radio show called *My Story of America* based on his best-selling book *My Story of America: Inspirational Stories of Life, Liberty and the Pursuit of Happiness*. This book chronicles the lives of eight ordinary people he interviewed who are modern-day heroes with extraordinary life experiences. It is the first book of the *My Story of America* series, which highlights the Judaeo-Christian principles of America's founding. An affirmative and inspiring work that has people nationwide excited and asking for more.

More information on Dr. George can be found at his website, MichaelTGeorge.com.